MEN'S RINGS

"This radiant world of metal and gems"

Charles Baudelaire, "The Jewels," *The Flowers of Evil*

YVES GASTOU

Photographs by Benjamin Chelly
Introduction and captions by Delphine Antoine
Texts by Harold Mollet

MEN'S RINGS

GINGKO PRESS

L'ÉCOLE, School of Jewelry Arts

TABLE OF CONTENTS

Editor's note: all quotations in the photo captions are from Yves Gastou.

Some encounters reveal unsuspected kinships. The one that brought us together with Yves Gastou signaled the beginning of a fruitful dialogue which culminated in the outstanding exhibition in October 2018 at L'ÉCOLE, School of Jewelry Arts of his incredible collection of men's rings. To accompany that one-of-a-kind show, it is our pleasure to sponsor the publication of this book with the hope that a larger audience will be able to discover Gastou's entire collection.

At the heart of the school's various missions is a desire to display jewelry in its myriad forms and expose little-known treasures. Founded in 2012 with the support of Van Cleef & Arpels, the school offers the general public the chance to gain knowledge of the history of jewelry and even gemology through different classes, workshops, exhibitions and conferences, both in Paris and around the world.

Always on the lookout for the personalities in the world of decorative arts, how could we not be charmed by Yves Gastou's life and career, warm personality, and unrivaled collection? Presented here are more than a thousand men's rings in a unique assortment that is multi-themed, eclectic, and profoundly unusual in its diversity.

Gastou is a habitué of Paris's greatest jewelers but the collection presented here explores new horizons. Whether silver or bejeweled, sober or extravagant, ceremonial or rebellious, his pieces are all marked by the extraordinary taste of a voracious gallery owner sampling freely from different eras and styles. From the bishop's rings he flaunts during Parisian suppers

to melancholy *memento mori*, Yves Gastou zigzags through history, casting light on the symbolic power of men's jewelry, its subtle meanings and ostentatious nature. Often eclipsed by women's ornamentation, the man's ring is resurrected here in an abundance that speaks to the eye, the soul, and the heart. Gastou's collection is alive and constantly evolving, worn to match life's moods and experiences. It is poignant, as well, through its simultaneously intimate and universal character. The collection is a reflection of an unusual personality, but also of a curiosity for beauty and mystery. This collection and these pages reveal the essence of what jewelry is—unsettling, diverse, and inseparable from the paths of men.

Marie Vallanet
President of L'ÉCOLE, School of Jewelry Arts

Nicolas Bos
President of Van Cleef & Arpels

INTRODUCTION

"Show me your ring, and I will tell you who you are..."

Yves Gastou: a collection as self-portrait

With his white hair and black suit, his dark glasses and noticeable rings, Yves Gastou is an unmissable personality of Saint-Germain-des-Prés, the neighborhood where he has lived and worked for more than 30 years. The man makes an impression. He is complex, a combination of strength and fragility, of lyricism and melancholy. His gallery is well-known, famous for its Ettore Sottsass-designed *terrazzo* façade, a scandal in the 1980s now become iconic, and a story already told in *Antiquaire du futur*[1]. His living spaces are also remarkable: from his apartment alongside the Seine—the very building where the troubled love affair between George Sand and Alfred de Musset occurred—to his house in Biarritz, a neo-troubadour hideaway and the home for his multiple collections. Despite the fact that Gastou is so well-known and usually willing to speak of himself, he turns out to be more reticent when asked about the reasons that compel him to collect. Suddenly, he becomes enigmatic, throwing out snippets of information like puzzle pieces. As we assemble them, the ghost of an answer appears. A man of instinct rather than analysis, introspection isn't really

his thing. Amid the new adventures, the constantly ringing telephone and a visitor-filled gallery, the question arises that maybe this is the only way he knows to keep boredom at bay, to remind himself he's still alive, still loved, still where he should be, and that he'll never be forgotten. But faced with the man who is always-on-the-go, running here and dashing there, it's easy to wonder what he might be running after. What lies behind his jovial and mischievous art dealer's mask?

A close look at his collection of rings reveals much of this mystery. Gastou's collection is excessive and impassioned—much like him. It is a reflection of the man himself. The collection remained unknown for so long. He never considered exhibiting his collection—no staged viewings at home or in his gallery, no museum displays—and he didn't bother inventorying them either. That is not his style. That would be much too methodical, too orderly, too tedious for the laconic treasure hunter that he is. His style is more impulsive and emotional. The rings are his most representative collection. With their recurring themes and repeated symbols, they are a part of him—the most beautiful and deepest part, the ones he has unrestrainedly gifted himself and calls "his loves".

Not at all a conservative collector, Yves finds his pleasure in creative collecting. He composes, reappropriates genres, and mixes fine jewelry with costume jewelry. The collection surprises with its diversity; from surrealism to eroticism, like his very curious acrylic ring (p. 153) with its combination of vanitas skull and fellatio, to the nobleman's signet ring with its family crest and hunting dogs, and the fantasy creatures, the Episcopal rings, the biker collection, as well as the ethnic, gothic, or designer pieces. Of all the collections he's assembled throughout his life—Art Nouveau, Art Deco, art of the 1940-1950-1970s, Neoclassical bronzes from the 19th century, the religious objects, the Joan of Arcs, the very street art Japanese *toys*, the stones patiently collected on the Ilbarritz beach, his secret garden—his collection of men's rings remains undoubtedly the most personal. The themes that mark the collection and the intimate use he makes of it, wearing them day after day, are a reflection of him. No matter how lavish, no matter how multifaceted, the collection is a self-portrait. And so it is the eclectic portrait, the rings themselves, who will do the confessing and speak for him.

Yves Gastou is both a contradiction to and the perfect embodiment of his gallery, a mix of high French taste and Baroque fantasy, just like his fashion style of Parisian chic spiced with biker rings, both elegant and provocative. His gallery will possibly be under construction, with his never-ending set-ups that last the entire day, doors open, the coming and going of deliveries, orders and re-orders, loud and exhausting, a dissonant ensemble that will only come together with the flick of the exulted conductor's baton. An exercise Yves claims to hate but truly must love because nothing is worse for him than inaction. For him, immobility very quickly equals boredom, emptiness, and stress. You will see him there, cursing and whinnying and stamping his foot. His stubborn and rooted Southern French accent, which he's retained for all these years, will surprise you until you see it for what it is: a brand that makes him the most Parisian of Southerners.

To really understand the collector, you have to go back to his childhood because according to him, "Everything began in Carcassonne."

Yves Gastou's life is like something out of a novel, with its protagonist somewhere between Peter Pan, and Eugène de Rastignac with his winner's energy and the power to turn a life into a destiny. Yves is that quintessential provincial who "makes it" in Paris. A born actor and a little bit of a ham, he's happy to take the center stage during a meal because of his rings, which draw listeners toward him and become conversation pieces. Don't all collectors wield the object to garner attention?

His story begins in Limoux, a small town of 10,000 inhabitants near Carcassonne. A child of the baby boom, he grew up with a loving mother. She was beloved by her four children. Yves often says, "My mother was always my accomplice. She bought me my first silver ring when I was seven or eight years old in Figueras, Spain, where we had gone on vacation. As a teenager she bought me my first signet ring with my initials, "YG" engraved, and also a *gourmette*[2] with Yves in large letters. It's horrible when I think about it now!" It is because of this mother who never said no, who tried her best to manage his contrarian nature, that he became an early collector. Yves remembers, "My mother had to buy me something every day or else I would throw a fit." The mother and son were intensely close, and as Yves likes to tell, he asked her every day for the same

thing, "Just another snuggle, Maman". He is as tactile with people as he is with objects, this need will
never leave him. The first thing he does when he re-
turns from scouring the markets is to wash the thing
he's purchased because, as he confesses, "There is
nothing more sensual." A ring as a parable of eroticism, as the fusion of the hand and the object, like
two bodies making love, this is exactly the idea that
Gastou presents when he explains his love for a given
ring simply because it suits him, "like a glove, like
a second skin". "I think that rings, more than necklaces or bracelets, signify union and sexuality." And,
as he often declares, "Wearing a ring is such a thrill,
because a ring is what we give to a fiancé, it's about
union. Giving a ring is a token of love."

His romantic, even lyric, vision of the ring makes
it a metaphor for the kindred soul, the gold or silver
unbreakable connection between two beings united
by one passion.

This unconventional mother-son relationship
would give him a forward-thinking vision, and the
strength of love. He ditched school regularly, most
often in the afternoons because the setting sun
made him melancholy. Clearly, rigid structures were
not for him. His mother, Odette, understood this and
believed that the child who helped her set the most
beautiful tables, who put together a stunning Christ-
mas tree had promising skills that would definitely
blossom if given the right patch of garden in which
to grow. She followed her intuition and placed him
with an antique dealer in Carcassonne. He remembers, "Everything begins with my apprenticeship to
Monsieur Thomas. I went into all of the houses, the
manors and castles. I accompanied him to estate
sales and I got my first ring when I was sixteen." And
so it was that young Yves found his way and began
to buy rings becoming a burgeoning collector.

An autodidact, he left school happily at the
age of sixteen. The rest is history. Carcassonne,

Toulouse, Saint-Ouen, and then quickly Paris. Yves
always sees further, sees bigger. And over time, the
previously bad student became one of the greatest antique dealers of his generation. His thirst for
culture and innate curiosity has only grown over
the years. He feeds it with books, plays, exhibitions,
opera, travel, and the human contact he has forged
with his customers as well as decorators, artists,
dealers, and journalists.

His father was a bailiff and auctioneer, and often
absent, which made for a more distant relationship.
Opposite his mother's overflowing love, his father
was a severe counterweight, a paternal barricade
which Yves's rebellious character would bump up
against. "From my father, I have kept the Friday sales
in the covered markets of Limoux that he prepared
until two or three o'clock in the morning. All the
women in town came to see Master Gastou for his
sales. He sold things that came from the large prop-
erties. All of these objects fascinated me—pen cases
or Gallé furniture, all from these families who had
once been rich and had now lost everything. I was
born with this refinement. From my mother, it was
Thursday afternoons. She loved everything: literature,
music, flowers, jewelry... She had incredible taste."
Thus, his parents left him a shared heritage, the taste
for beautiful things and a love of esthetics. It is very
moving, as well, when Yves confides that his father,
incapable of giving him the smallest compliment,
admitted at the end of his life that he'd saved every
press clipping, had snipped and organized every
magazine on the Biennial into a folder as if to honor
the enfant terrible he'd never understood.

Between 1975 and 1980, Yves's ring collection grew,
but things really sped up after he established himself in Paris, first opening a flea market stall in 1981
and then a gallery on the rue Bonaparte in 1985.

He contacted all the great Parisian jewelry houses, especially Mellerio dits Meller, the official supplier for the high clergy and aristocracy. At this shop, he discovered cases overflowing with gleaming bishops' rings waiting to be broken down for their parts. If Yves had not purchased them, each stone would have been removed from its setting, and the metal would have been melted down, all of these masterpieces would have disappeared without a trace. His interest in forgotten objects, whether religious or decorative, remains a fundamental element of his approach as a collector: "Seeing all these magnificent objects lying about on the ground when they had once been cared for, cleaned, put away in a dresser... it's impossible for me to just leave them there, so I buy them and when they belong to me, I clean them and then I organize them into cases." He has always been interested in stray objects, something once-loved and then forgotten. For Yves, antiquing has always been a way of giving life back to an object. This vocation—part redemptive, part animistic—is what had him scouring the boutiques in Les Halles and the Marais on the hunt for his biker rings and those extraordinary bracelets and necklaces, whether Hells Angels or hippie, that in the 1980s had become outdated when fashion turned more towards the punk and new wave styles. He was reminded of the pop stars he'd admired in the 1960s and 1970s: Johnny Halliday, Mick Jagger, and even Elvis Presley. And it was his focus on men's rings that eventually brought him to women's jewelry. At the beginning, he was interested in the 1940s and 1950s, from Boivin to Belperron, and then turned to the 1970s with Jean Vendome and Andrew Grima, and he slowly amassed a tremendous collection that was as fascinating as it was detrimental. He admits, "It's an illness that sometimes means I put myself in danger." Hearing him, it is clear that his collection is nothing more than an addiction

for the object, an obsessive tendency to accumulate. He stopped collecting women's jewelry in the early 2000s after a painful personal separation, and this prompted a return again to men's rings. At that point, his collection increased exponentially. The act of collecting also took on a new dimension. This is when Gastou began to wear his rings every day, all categories mixed together, from a biker ring to an Episcopal ring, whereas before he was stubborn about wearing bishop's rings only periodically for private dinners. And so his famous pairings came to life, and the ring became an essential accessory of his persona, granting him a glamorous, rock and roll image that would remain wedded to his brand. The ring witnessed the rebirth of a personality as he rediscovered the 1970s, overturning the 1940s and 50s neoclassical glitzy style of his former life. His taste for provocation and reclaiming symbols, and in line with the "Gastounian" art of exploding accepted codes allows him to get carried away in his favorite game: upending the tables. That upheaval accomplished, he then re-deals the cards, daring the most improbable combinations, but ones which, on his hand, take on a particular meaning. And so Yves concocted what the media often calls, "Gastou style," his signature combination of chic and shock.

Yves childhood home also forged his character as a collector. He describes it as Cathar country, rebellious and mysterious. After growing up in the shadow of Medieval Carcassonne, he will always associate the city with the neo-troubadour vitality of the architect Viollet-le-Duc. For Yves Carcassonne symbolizes the fort and the battlements, the drawbridge, the white Knights and the troubadours—the entire medieval fable and its many enchanting elements: sensitive virility, courtly love, bravery, the code of honor. For Gastou, the Middle Ages are also connected to the crusades and

Christianity's oscillation between the sword and the cross. His collection reveals his fascination for the gothic dawn of the Hundred Years War as embodied in the androgynous Joan of Arc with her shining breastplate; "Armor is so beautiful, it's like a shell. This is why I've idolized Joan of Arc since I was 15. Joan is androgyny. I've always loved androgyny, like Mick Jagger and David Bowie."

Carcassonne also symbolizes the crown. As a child on holiday with his mother in Spain, the crown meant the ones he saw in churches atop the heads of Mary, of Jesus, and all the saints, a symbol of love, generosity, power, and eternity. Later, Freddy Mercury would awaken his admiration by appropriating this object as the symbol for Queen. He remembers, "On TV, I watched him enter the stage with his bare chest and his ermine cape. And then he put the crown! Incredible beauty!"

Childhood memories crystallized forever in the flamboyant gemstones of the clergy of the past; they are his Proustian madeleine. In the beginning of the 1960s, the entire family went every Sunday to mass at St. Martin's church. This was a traditional, Southern style mass, "...with incense, singing, music on a large organ, processions, the emotion, and the beauty". And then came his fall from grace, encapsulated in the following anecdote which he has so many times repeated: "At the end of mass, I went to kiss the hand of the Bishop as was the tradition, except that I went back two or three times, and finally my mother caught me and asked me why I was doing this. I told her: 'But, Maman, he has such a beautiful ring!'" His first dip into a bottomless well. His religion as a collector stands in for any real faith: "I don't believe in God, but I believe in human ingenuity. When I see these masterpieces, paintings, sculptures, architectures, I am fascinated by

these works dedicated to God," he confides. Gastou possesses about one hundred bishop's rings—masterpieces of goldsmithing and set with precious and semi-precious stones—forming a cornerstone that is the most intimate but also the most spectacular part of his collection.

The *memento mori*, literally "remember that you must die" is also a major theme. Generally represented by the vanitas skulls, there are also other related motifs, like crosses or coffins, always linked somehow to the idea of death. When asked about the origins of this tendency, Yves is long-winded: "When I was young and there was a death in my town near Carcassonne or in Spain in Figueras or in Cadaqués, they would hang a large cloth of honor in front of the door of the deceased person's home, and gold or silver thread would draw the skull and initials inside a heraldic shield. There was also a pulpit covered in black and a book that everyone signed. At that time, in the 1950s, there were several categories of burial: first, second, and third class depending on the deceased's status. In St. Martin's church where I spent my days, I skulked about the sacristy to see the objects that were used for each of these categories. And then in the church again, there was the great statue of Christ on the cross that would be covered in black for the funeral. I also remember the old hearses covered in a black baldaquin and drawn by horses all decked out with ostrich feathers and priests wearing a black chasuble embroidered with silver. All of this definitely left an impression on me. France at the time, the France of my childhood, was still the 19th century!" Thus explained, the entire spirit of the collection can be seen. From his coffin or cross rings, to his vanitas skulls, death in all its forms is omnipresent. An extremely personal way of confronting life by accepting death as an integral part of it. To conjure up one's last moments by dressing up

Yves Gastou (right) and his son Victor (above).

in its finery, a little like Mexico's *fiesta de los muertos*, means coming to terms with death by celebrating it as a hymn to life. Yves confides, "I could let it all go from one day to the next. Start all over. This is what I learned from my maternal grandfather, who was Spanish and an anarchist."

Yves is also attracted to objects of mourning. Is this an homage to the actress Sarah Bernhardt, his adolescent idol, who slept inside coffins? Certainly, but not exclusively. The attachment to this particular category of his collection also comes from his broader admiration for everything surrounding death, his beloved religious music, especially requiems—*The Mass for Rossini*, in particular—and films. He even confesses that the burial scene of the child in Kubrick's *Barry Lyndon* always makes him cry. Cemeteries or churches remain what he calls the space of the irrational and they continue to inhabit him. "When I was 14 years old, I didn't play soccer or rugby with my friends. I didn't like that. I didn't feel comfortable in such a masculine environment. I have always preferred women or more occult places like the churches, cemeteries, or castles I explored as a child and a teenager." He remembers a difficult period of his life, "In Paris, in 2004, just after my divorce, I would go walking in cemeteries, mostly Père Lachaise and Montmartre, this was very good for me... It was in Montmartre actually that I bought some biker rings because of the skulls. At that time, I was wearing only vanitas skulls." His love of art, of beauty is a way for him to re-glue life's broken pieces, dance on death's grave and to reconcile with himself and with life.

His collection abounds with an entire gothic bestiary – nods to *Alien*, *Predator*, space monsters, and ox skulls. Yves explains that the monsters go back to the flying saucer films of 1950s American cinema,

which nurtured his youth with their surreal papier mâché astronaut costumes. In the 1980s, he would fall for Ridley Scott's science fiction. As a child, Yves climbed into bell towers to admire the gargoyles strange and mysterious shapes. Baudelaire wrote that, "Beauty is always bizarre." Yves's bestiary is also inspired by his discoveries in *The Adventures of Tintin* comic books. The ox skull that he took for his gallery's logo certainly came out of the decorative tradition of the 1970s which he rediscovered in the 2000s. But the ox skull is also about the corrida, the bloody ritual marriage between man and bull, the myth of the Minotaur. The matador with his flirtatious suit of light is poised between masculine and feminine, symbolizing the transvestite. An androgyny that has always influenced Gastou, certainly because it reminds him of the Limoux carnival and its satire, which he finds more interesting than its larger cousin in Venice: "I loved the particular moment that we could see the mayor disguised as a woman. Everyone always wanted to dress me up as Pierrot, with the crying face and wide trousers. As a teenager I often dressed up as a woman. I tried on my mother's dresses, put on her nylons, and I wore her jewelry." Yet another example of his endless contradictions and their dose of provocation.

Another significant element of his collection are his ethnic rings, memories of his treasure hunting travels. He considers a trip a success if he can bring something back. Vast open landscapes are not for him, he prefers the material vestiges of the civilizations that have passed on, objects he can look at, touch, and eventually buy. Nothing makes him happier than visiting a temple, a church, a mosque or museum, scouring old boutiques to discover some forgotten piece, and then strolling through a souk or a flea market. This is what he does wherever he goes—in Germany, in Spain, in Malta. Once, on a trip to Rome, he ransacked a shop near the Pantheon that sold religious trinkets, going behind the counters to search frenetically through every single drawer while the confused salesperson looked on, worried he was maybe dealing with a crazy person. He did the same in Casablanca, where he bought a stock of 90 ethnic rings. With his usual focus on beauty and aesthetics, Gastou tells us about his travels: "Arab men are magnificent in their turbans, and they look wonderful in their djellaba. They have the noble and majestic attitude to suit it. From a simple chauffeur in Marrakesh or a temple guard at Abou Simbel, to the Middle Eastern princes, they're all elegant. And they wear rings. So when I see them I think I have the right to have some, too."

His collection also includes sculpture rings, either tribal or designer, creating an interesting analogy with the designer furniture in his gallery. He explains, "My African rings are like small sculptures on a band. They are like little Giacometti's. They are not worth so much, but I love looking at them." One is tempted to ask him why sculpture instead of painting? His response is not surprising, "Because sculpture is tactile, you can touch it. Painting is abstract, it's flat, it's not really for me." This shows us once again the man he really is, more emotional than cerebral, and for whom, as Anatole France wrote, "In art as in love, instinct is enough."

This mixture of costume jewelry and luxury infuses the entire collection. He has an immense capacity to look for and love both the smallest objects and the big ones, and this he gets from his mother and his father. An improbable cocktail which certainly enabled him to see things differently, giving him an extraordinary freedom to think outside of customary frameworks. Which is exactly what he admires in an atypical personality like Pope Francis who chose

white robes with a simple cross and a small silver band. Yves completely loves this, "I knew blue-collar priests. In my collection of bishop's and priest's rings, I also have very simple models, very refined, made with poor quality materials, but just as creative." A large part of his collection celebrates the enlightened mindset of clergy like Father Couturier who got the great artists and jewelers just after the Second World War to infuse France's religious art with modernity.

Finding solace in beauty—isn't this precisely the collector's gift? "I experience the same feeling when looking at an exquisitely decorated chateau as I do when seeing a fisherman's cottage in Cadaqués where we visited with my mother, so beautiful and extremely clean. When I hear an oratorio or requiem by a 200-member choir, I cry; but I feel just as much emotion in a bistro with an accordion player and a singer." In both journeys, as an art dealer and as a collector, his approach has remained the same: "...to see what other people don't see." This means choosing an object for itself and not for its sales value. "I'm not looking for something valuable just because it's a diamond or a ruby! I don't care about that at all! I look for something I think is exceptional because it gives me an emotion, whether it's a fifty Euro biker ring, a silver ring with a Heart of Jesus, or a bishop's ring with pearls and precious stones." Gastou's motto has always been to buy with one's heart, forcing emotion to triumph over rational investment. "The hand of God, baraka." No matter the words, we understand what has always motivated him, a faith in himself and in life. An eternal optimist, Yves Gastou is a happy man. He knows that he's lived his passion and is still living it.

Gastou has always been ahead of the times and his vision has never faltered. This pioneering spirit is exactly what he's always praised in the great designers like Karl Lagerfeld, Yves Saint Laurent, Christian Lacroix, Chantal Thomass, and Sonia Rykiel, and they were all some of the first clients of his Parisian gallery. These avant-garde talents also brought forgotten styles back to the center stage, like Pierre Cardin, an immense rediscover of art nouveau. They spoke the same language and immediately understood each other. Amassed over more than 30 years, his ring collection fully represents his pioneering artistic quest. He admits that back in the day it was the rare man who dared to wear jewelry, and at the risk of being labeled, "a poof" or "trashy" or "gay", a trend that today has been completely reversed. Just look at male fashion. There isn't a single big brand and designer that doesn't offer men's jewelry. Gastou is extremely proud of this. He praises this new generation because they "finally have the intelligence and courage to accept their feminine side, to recognize the bisexual esthetic, finally after all these years!" He loves this democratization of luxury and how masculine elegance has re-infiltrated society—from Martin Margiela to Rick Owens at Zara, and from Marc Jacobs to Nicolas Ghesquère at Uniqlo. With a nearly childish joy and a smile of inner satisfaction, he watches this evolution on the streets.

He never hesitates to show his enthusiasm when he notices a ring on someone's finger, stepping forward to casually ask, "What's your ring, where's it from?" He also likes how the new generation validates its own choices, normalizing and affirming them, wearing its choices as he wears his rings: as an identity, like a nobleman proudly sporting his heraldic crest, the woman with her diamonds, or the biker with his silver skulls. With some mischief, he even goes a step further, praising the hip hop style of American rappers like Kanye West or Rick Ross: "The way they drip with gold chains and rings and

furs makes them look just like those portraits of nobles under François I or Henry the 8th. Even if it's ridiculous, like the doges or the Popes could be, I think it's magnificent, amazing, masterfully provocative!" This speaks volumes about his own infatuation with the insolence of taste, where a combination of audacity and freedom create a kitsch that touches the sublime—all that he loves. He admires strong personalities who dare to be themselves and let their clothing and jewelry speak for who they are. He confesses being captivated by, "the handsome butcher or truck driver sporting his golden ring, his tattoos or his earring—always clues of a personality". He admires them, he insists, as much as the dandies of the 19th century like Boni de Castellane, Marcel Proust, and Oscar Wilde.

But beyond his innate sense for provocation, which he expertly wields—so much so that this has become the spearhead of his media image—it is clear that behind this he is deeply sincere. His attachment to otherness is compelling. With scathing humor, he tells the following story: "There was a boy who dreamed of meeting the Pope. When the day finally comes, he's delighted. He gets in front of the Pope and he kneels to kiss the Pope's hand, and he says, 'Your Holiness, what a beautiful ring you have!' The Holy Father leans toward him and says, 'I've got matching earrings, too, but they won't let me wear them!'" Going further, he says, "Don't forget that during Antiquity, in the Renaissance and the 19th and early 20th centuries, men wore gold hoop earrings in Corto Maltese style, and necklaces, and of course they wore rings. Today, in the 21st century, it's even more intense." For Gastou this doesn't mean society has banalized personal ornamentation, he prefers to think it represents an aestheticization of society. An idea which clearly pleases his non-conformist, libertine side, the man who championed this idea in his youth by adopting all manner of eccentric clothing styles that have, with maturity, been replaced by his rings. From his Belle Epoque cape, to his Jean Ferrat mustache, and all that came in between—the riding boots, the berets and hats, his vintage Jaguar with a beturbaned skull on the hood instead of a hood ornament—he dared nearly everything by never forbidding himself anything. His brave choices, undertaken even while still a young antique dealer only beginning to garner attention, are what comprise his character. He remains an eternal assailant of the fortress of good taste.

Gastou is a man of immediacy, a zapper who wants everything to go quickly. He feels in line with today's cosmopolitan and always-in-motion society in which feminine values, love, and sentiment have triumphed. He agrees with Aragon and Ferrat that the woman is man's future. When discussing today's young men, like his son Victor, he admires their freedom of style expressed with their long hair, their jewelry, their beards and their tattoos. He likes this new deal in which originality has become the norm. Here again, the future proves him right, and this is maybe the key to the mystery of Yves Gastou, the paradox of the man who is an old-style art dealer hunting treasures one by one, going every Friday to the flea market like he has always done, resistant to emails, texts, preferring direct contact over indirect machine-mediated connections. He is a kind of dinosaur in today's international, cyber-based art world. At the same time, he is a renowned gallery owner brimming with new ideas and new projects. Yves Gastou, antiquarian of the future: the perfect euphemism to define him. He embodies both extremes of the same creative universe, exploring the past to reinvent the future.

If aesthetics, background, and culture influence and explain the act of collecting, so do the psychological forces at work within the collector. What remains now is to wonder what Yves Gastou now expects from his collection? "Nothing more than what it has given me," he confidently responds. He could be speaking of a romantic relationship, and indeed, he is someone who loves his things and his homes with the same affection and sincerity as he might love a woman. In any case, his collection—gathered piece by piece, day after day—comes together to create his self-portrait. But to hear him speak about it, the portrait seems to be nearly complete and when it is, he predicts the following: "When the book comes out, I'll collect a few more pieces, and then I'll get rid of a large portion of my rings because I have other collecting to do…"

All that remains then is to relinquish them. Sell. Throw his dreams high into the air so that others will catch them. That is the fate of any collection. To die in order to be reborn. And then the circle will be complete.

DELPHINE ANTOINE

1   From the title of Delphine Antoine's book, *Yves Gastou antiquaire du future*, (Yves Gastou, Antiquary of the future), Paris, Editions Norma, 2011.
2   In France a "gourmette" is a braided chain bracelet with a smooth flat medallion on one side bearing the first name of the wearer. Similar to an American-style ID bracelet.

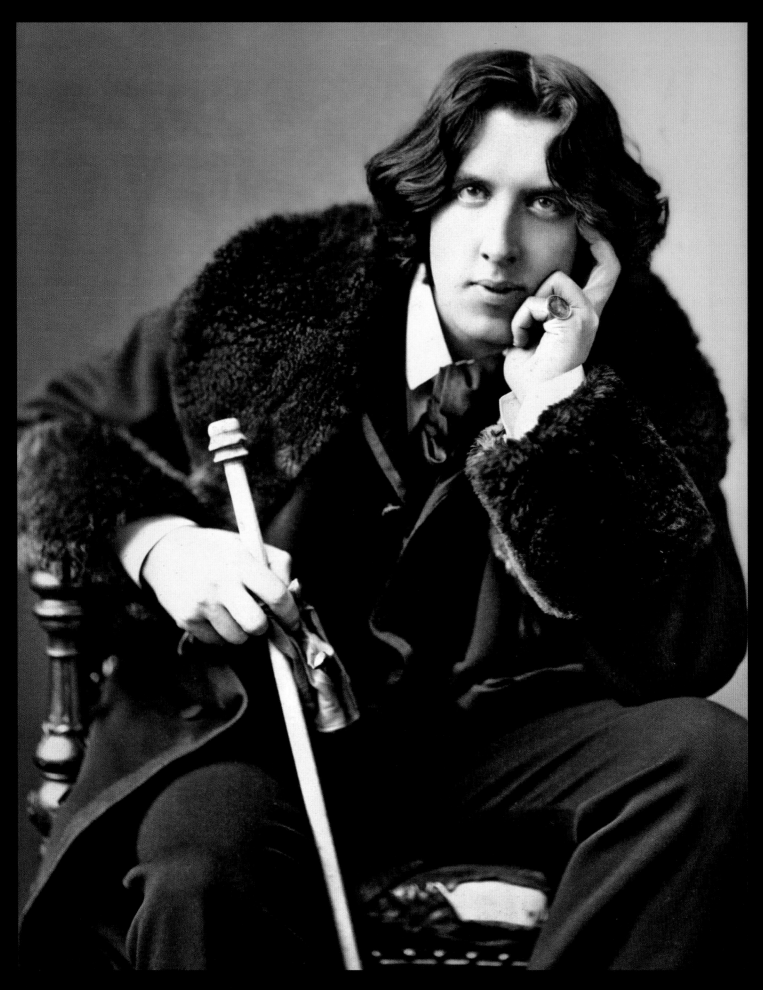

Rings subtly reveal the history of men. Like the signet ring, that singular example of masculine pomp, which has spanned the ages and ornamented the hands of the greats with its splendor.

Reserved for the highest dignitaries of ancient Egypt, the signet was decorated with scarabs, divine figures, and hieroglyphs. The Greeks, the Etruscans, and the Romans all used them, customizing to suit their codes. As time passed, signets were decorated with new bestiaries and new gods. Their adornments were inspired by founding mythologies and featured allegories, dreams, and heroes. Their gold and silver settings were adorned with intaglios, engraved hollows that played upon the transparency of fines stones, as well as cameos with their craftmanship in relief that exposed the layers of changing colors of the cabochon. The faces stand out from the creamy white of their pastel planes while the marbled veins delicately heighten the drawing. Philosophers, emperors, and generals can be found in profile, sacred stone figures rendered sublime by their artistic delicacy.

The thinkers and theoreticians of the European Enlightenment were thirsty for knowledge and dipped into ancient literatures to re-center themselves at the source of all art. The discoveries and archaeological digs at major sites in Italy, Greece, and Asia minor opened the path to developing the foundations of neoclassicism. This was the heyday of the "Grand Tour": to complete their cultural education, the youth of wealthy families travelled for several months across the continent, returning with numerous art objects from the great civilizations of antiquity. From the North Sea to the Aegean, aesthetes, collectors, architects, and artists crossed paths and exchanged their stories. Lord Byron's letters to his mother tell of his travels in great detail. Berlioz creates a marvelous symphony from his journey. Tischbein paints Goethe lounging in the Italian countryside, to his right a bas-relief partially covered with ivy and an Ionic capital; behind him the ruins of an

aqueduct and fort. Graceful postures inhabit the figures in painting from David to Ingres. Arching naked bodies in white marble statues. These travel memories, the publications that accompanied them, and the learned societies participating in the distribution of the Greek, Roman, and Etruscan canons gave rise to neoclassical aesthetics which then spread to every artistic domain.

And thus appeared signet rings on aristocratic hands; the Three Graces with perfectly draped robes, a helmeted Hermes, Plato, and warrior Athena surrounded by acanthus leaves and geometric friezes. Antique coins find new life in new settings. Intaglio rings circulate between England, Germany, and France. They are ordered via catalogue, reproduced, and feverishly collected. The Englishman James Tassie, considered one of the most prolific collectors and gem merchants of the 18th century, amassed entire planks of molds for reproducing these designs. Number 1493 of the inventory created by his nephew William Tassie is a cherub seated on the shoulders of a devil beneath the words, "The devil carries love away" (p. 26). Alongside these fantasy images and frivolous decorations, the ring was also political. In France, for example, were busts of a young, long-haired Napoleon in his general's uniform, with a serene and victorious face like Antoine-Jean Gros's painting, *Bonaparte at the Pont d'Arcole* (p. 35).

Further celebrated by the Ecole and Academy des Beaux-Arts, various successive neoclassical styles crossed the 19th century and continued to be explored until the first half of the 20th century. The selection presented here show the echoes in Yves Gastou's taste for the decorative architecture and decors of the 1940s. Like André Arbus embellishing his furniture with the faces of antiquity sculpted by Vadim Androusov, Gastou surrounds himself with these classical marvels of men's jewelry.

Harold Mollet

Left: Ring, carnelian intaglio with inset of a child's portrait in the style of Dauphin Louis XVII or a Roman king, encircled with guilloché yellow gold and royal blue enamel, late 18th century. **Right:** Intaglio rings of carnelian, garnet, and agate, neoclassical settings in yellow gold and silver, 19th century. Clockwise: profile of a bearded man (beards were a symbol of warriors and noblemen, also of wisdom and strength in ancient Greece), centaur, profile of Diadumenos (athlete bearing the victor's headband), standing figure engraved in a half-moon antique stone and set in an exceptional Etruscan style, profile of neoclassical helmeted warrior, warrior Athena (helmet, lance, shield), sacred cow, late 18th and 19th centuries.

Left: Refined taste. Rings for the learned gentleman, yellow gold, carnelian intaglio rings, yellow gold and vermeil, middle of the 19th century. Upper left: angel with ithyphallic devil, engraved with words, "the devil carries love away", shoulder embossed with rosettes and shells, French craftsmanship, circa 1850. Upper right: ram engraved on stone, Charles X setting. Lower left: helmeted warrior in a Renaissance style, ring embossed with plant motifs. Lower right: engraved winged victory **Right:** Cameos and intaglios, yellow gold. Clockwise: portrait of Blaise Pascal, onyx, polygonal setting, 18th century; carnelian intaglio featuring Apollo, 19th century; white agate cabochon encircled with black, 1900; men's portraits in antique brown agate veined with white and carnelian agate with neoclassical man's head with laurel crown, 19th century. Center: cameo ring, a *putto* riding Triton, metal, late 18th century.

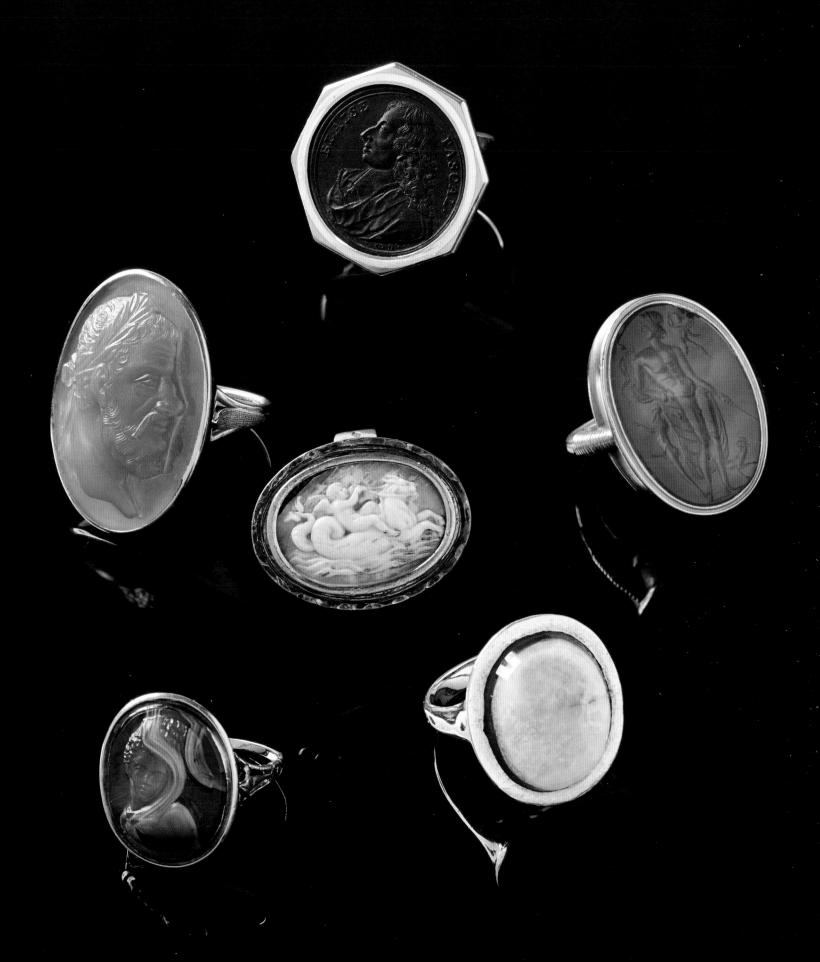

Left: Magnetic Mirror. Foreground: vermeil ring, enameled portrait on silver, late 18th century-early 19th century. Center: enameled skull, jeweled and decorated with multicolor butterflies on each side, silver, Mexican craftsmanship. Background: nobleman's ring, miniature on porcelain, portrait of a nobleman in a wig, signed and dated, Johann Friedrich Ardin, 1714. **Right:** Antiquity Exhumed. Clockwise: signet with coat-of-arms, 20th century; cameo with profile of Diadumenos, circa 1900; silver ring depicting the God Hermes (winged helmet), 1900; signet ring—seal—depicting Triton, silver, 1950–1960; antique Roman coin reset into a silver ring and melted, Italian craftsmanship, 19th century; Etruscan ring, silver, antique stone in onyx, 1930s.

Left: Masculine Elegance. Cameo rings, yellow gold and vermeil. Clockwise: Baroque setting embossed with plant motifs, profile of Isis with vulture headdress, late 18th century-early 19th century; highly accomplished studded hexagonal setting, cameo of Perseus in profile, helmeted and carrying a shield, pink and white gold, 19th century; cameo ring, character from antiquity, 19th century. **Right:** Grand Tour Souvenirs. Top: onyx intaglio ring featuring the Three Graces, silver, 19th century. Center: left, Art Deco signet ring, carnelian agate, silver, 1930; right: ring, antique coin with king's profile, openwork floral motif on the shoulders, Armenia, circa 1920–1930. Bottom: portraits of neoclassical bearded men, silver, 19th century.

Left: Bezel ring with St. Luke's winged bull; silver ring with blazon; 8-sided pyramidal Renaissance ring, set with sapphire cabochon, vermeil, England, 13th century. Lower left: medieval ring, St. Mark's lion engraved beneath a Greek cross pattée, vermeil, 13th–14th century. Right: hunter's ring, tooth inset into the embossed silver setting. **Right:** La Piovra, Sicilian mafia. Below the octopus buckle of the American belt and moving clockwise: ring in yellow gold, band embossed with flowers and set with a blood jasper, England, 19th century; oriental ring, granulated gold and carnelian agate; yellow gold ring, citrine, Italy, 1900.

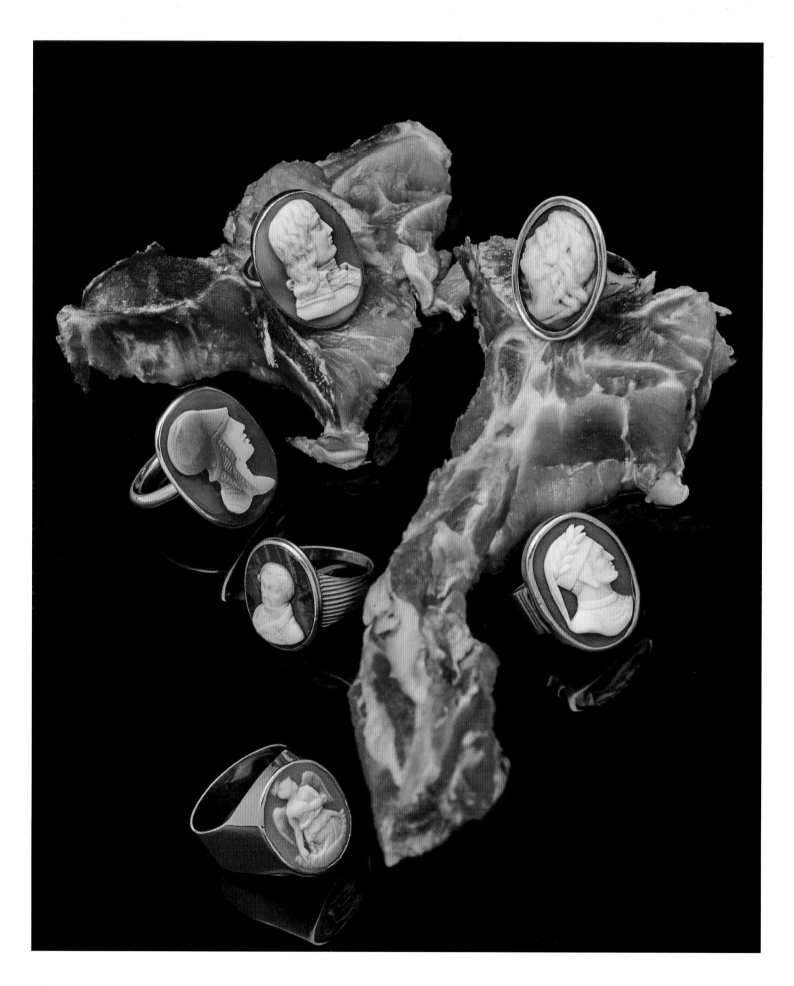

Left: Serene Highness. *Doge* bezel ring that opens to conceal a dose of poison, oval carnelian intaglios, decorated with leaves and stylized coat-of-arms of the *doges* of Venice, symbols of Venetian rule, silver and metal, 19th century. **Right:** In the flesh. Rings for noblemen and upper bourgeoisie, neoclassical style, featuring profiles of famous men like Bonaparte or Dante, cameos, yellow gold and silver, late 18th century-early 19th century.

Left: Everlasting Love. Rings for snips of hair, love tokens. Hair locket promise rings, gold leaf engravings bearing the inscription, "Ils sont unis pour la vie" (They are united for life), (left), stencil and painted parchment paper with the words, "Amour-Constance-Amitié-Confiance" (Love-Faithfulness-Friendship-Trust) and an obelisk topped with a firepot and the initial "L" (right), pink gold, Romantic era, France, circa 1820. **Right:** Happy Widow. Top: orthodox rings, Russia. Lower middle: mourning rings, metal, gold, cameos, miniatures of the deceased, England, late 18th century-early 19th century.

2

CHIVALRY

Symbols of belonging and recognition, the signet rings presented here were signifiers of identity and social position.

These rings were passed down from one generation to the next, privileged witnesses of family histories. Beginning in the 11th century, the heraldry marking a knight's armor were used to ease their identification on a battlefield. These coats-of-arms decorated all of their equipment and were also engraved on rings that served as seals. They were designed according to the rules of heraldry. The shield, in the center, was divided into fields which featured the charges, geometric designs, and natural or imaginary figures like the fleur-de-lis, the cross, and the griffon. Exterior ornamentation completed the arms: supports, real or invented animals to either side of the shield, crown, helm and mantling on the upper part, motto and terrace on the lower part. Every noble title is codified, each function within the catholic and military hierarchy translated by a different ornament. The simpler blazons of the Middle Ages slowly gave way to busier, colored and more complex designs. Forbidden by decree in 1790 during the French Revolution, heraldic arms found a new visual language with the nobility of the First French Empire under Napolean I.

The rediscovery of Medieval architecture at the dawn of the 19th century imprinted an idealized vision of the era on the minds of the period. The Romantic movement adopted the troubadour style in its painting and decorative arts. Prosper Mérimée, who was inspector general of historical monuments at the time, was interested in the ruins of large architectural works. With a desire to give new value to France's national heritage, he mandated Eugène Viollet-le-Duc to restore numerous medieval buildings including the Mont-Saint-Michel, the city of Carcassonne, and Paris's Notre Dame Cathedral. Also, the widespread use of lithograph made it possible to distribute collections of engravings like the *Voyages pittoresques et romantiques dans l'ancienne France* (Picturesque and Romantic Travels through Old France) by Baron Taylor and Charles Nodier, which catalogued the landscapes and remarkable works of art from different French regions. This aesthetic universe also inspired goldsmiths, amongst whom François-Désiré Froment-Meurice is the greatest example. Victor Hugo even dedicated a poem to him (in *The Contemplations*) that likened the artist's metalwork to the finest poetry. Théophile Gautier also wrote a celebratory obituary of Froment-Meurice in *La Presse* after he died. The jeweler created exceptional pieces for his well-heeled clients, members of the clergy, and European heads of state. Gastou's collection includes a piece of his: a nobleman's heraldry in lapis-lazuli, held by two warriors and set in a finely embossed gold (p. 51). The coats of arms were done on silver, carnelian, agate and crystal. The bands themselves were either unadorned or richly decorated, like this assortment of hunting rings, adorned with hares (p. 50).

At the beginning of the 20th century, signet rings became a fashionable clothing accessory and were transformed into a social marker loaded with various symbolic meanings.

They were worn by dandies like Oscar Wilde, immortalized by Napoleon Sarony's photographs in 1882 (p. 22), and Balzac, as described by Léon Gozlan in a biography. The rings were highly prized by the artistic communities across Europe. They also became an integral part of American style, nicknamed the "pinky ring" for the finger upon which they were worn.

Cinema brought the signet to the mafia world: from Edward G. Robinson in Mervyn LeRoy's *Little Caesar* (1931) to Robert de Niro in Martin Scorcese's *Casino*, and even more recently with James Gandolfini in the series *The Sopranos*. The music industry adopted them as well. Crooners and Jazz musicians wore them solemnly, while eccentric icons like Liberace and Prince appropriated them to suit their own unique styles. Cantor of masculinity, the signet is now adopted by rappers like Puff Daddy and Rick Ross and displayed with an opulence nearly as flashy as the jewels worn in Renaissance era portraits.

Symbols of success and excellence, championship rings have been given to victorious sports teams in the United States since the 1930s—baseball's world series, the NASCAR cup, and the Super Bowl. The 2011 Green Bay Packers' ring (p. 60) is a perfect example: the four marquis cut diamonds represent the shape of the ball for the team's four Super Bowl wins, the "G" of the team's logo is set with 13 diamonds to represent its 13 NFL titles and the 92 diamonds for the franchise's 92 year-long history. The platinum and gold ring was created by Jostens, a company founded in 1897 that has specialized in class rings since the 1920s. A tradition that doesn't exist in France, to the great regret of Yves Gastou, class rings (p. 227) are meant for high school and university students, for academies and different military corps, and are signs of honor, belonging, and recognition. The tradition is used in Canada for engineers, and in Sweden and Denmark for Ph.D. students.

The signet is worn on the ring finger and its aura is just as powerful when worn by Franklin Roosevelt as it is by Prince Charles. A gift to boys when they become men, decorated with the family crest, initials, or left blank, the signet ring can be found in any social category, as much a symbol of virility as a sign of androgyny.

Yves Gastou's collection offers us a personal and eclectic selection of signet rings from the 19th century all the way through to today.

Harold Mollet

Left: The Time of the Crusades. Important ring, spectacular marquise cut amethyst, crusader's sword set into the stone and set with diamonds and rubies, crowns on the shoulder, claws and Roman cross decorating the bezel, motto engraved on the perimeter, "Vox populi, vox dei" (The voice of the people is the voice of God) in reference to the popular call to join the crusades launched by itinerant preachers, Lydia Courteille, one-of-a-kind, contemporary design. **Right:** "The city towers of my Carcassonne." Fortress ring, silver, circa 1900. It may also be a Jewish wedding ring.

Left: God served first. Assortment of five gold and silver rings. Designed and gifted by his beloved, these rings are cherished by the collector. From Joan of Arc's heraldry (sword, fleur-de-lis, and royal crown) to the suffering Christ, the crown of thorns, the fortress, and finally the Jesus heart, these rings embody the themes which Yves Gastou holds dear: the Passion and knighthood. At the origin of these affinities is the city of Carcassonne, his childhood home and where his imagination came to life. One-of-a-kind pieces, Philippe Niederländer, 2009 to 2013. **Right:** Incarnate. Signet rings with the heraldry of the great bourgeois families or counts, carnelian intaglios, blood jasper, crystal, citrine, embossed and engraved gold, 19th century. Far upper right, the motto, "He who believes gets to the heart of things," engraved into the jasper.

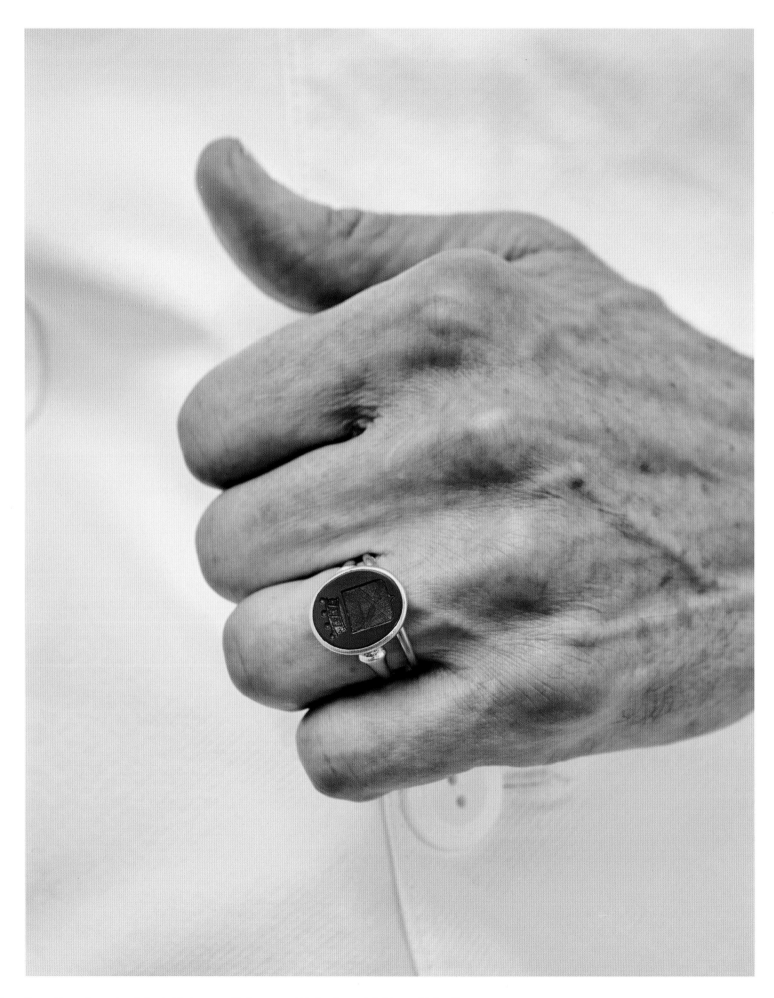

Baron X wearing a signet ring in black onyx with the arms of his family crest: Sable, or chief, saltire argent

Left: "Neo-troubadour rings, icon of Knighthood Richard the Lion Heart, and the Languedoc cross, all of my loves." Vanitas skull and cartouche rings, royal crown inset, silver and gold, Corpus Christi, circa 2010. Other rings, silver, synthetic gemstones. **Right:** Bottom: ring with mechanism, heart below a crown, silver. Middle: priest's ring, crucifixion, silver, 19th century; ring, fleur-de-lis, silver, Abraxas, 2000. Top: openwork Malta cross in relief, silver, Abraxas; enamel Gothic cross, Alchemy Gothic.

Left: The Hunt. Hunters' rings, counts' heraldry, jasper intaglio featuring neoclassical bearded man, wild boar and hunting dogs sculpted on the shoulders (hares, used for coursing), gold and vermeil, 19th century. **Right:** "Nothing is impossible for the valiant heart." Museum ring, personalized knights in armor rising up in high relief on the shoulder, heraldic intaglio in lapis-lazuli, embossed silver and vermeil, one-of-a-kind, Froment-Meurice, 19th century.

Left: "My entire universe of the Addams Family and the haunted or abandoned castles of my childhood can be seen in the dungeons of the city of Carcassonne." Upper left: opium ring, decorated with Asian dragon on the bezel, inscription inside the band: "Je respire profondément et sans crainte." (I breathe deeply and fearlessly.) Upper right: priest's ring, jasper engraved with the following inscription: "credo, amo, opero" (I believe, I love, I act), yellow gold, date engraved inside: 24 April 1845. Center: Recumbent effigy ring, metal, Alchemy Carta England, 1997. Bottom: two gothic rings, silver and synthetic gemstones, Gemmex Paris.

Right: Assortment of antique rings in silver, vermeil, enamel. Skull ring with the forehead marked with the Languedoc cross, Corpus Christi, 2013.

Left: Bonapartism. Signet ring, yellow gold setting made of fish scales in relief, inlaid with an agate intaglio detailing a shield under a cinquefeuille, symbol of European nobility, late 19ᵗʰ century. **Right:** Addams Family, *gentry* style. Noblemen's rings, amethyst, jasper, and citrine intaglio, gold and engraved silver, featuring heraldry and comital (upper left and right) or margravial crowns (left foreground), Baroque heraldry (upper left), foliate scroll pattern engraved on the band and citrine engraved with the patron's initials, 19ᵗʰ century.

Left: "The heavy weights of my collection. I love wearing them." Christ ring, La Mandragore. Three rings, gothic crosses and angels, solid silver, Chrome Hearts, 2014. **Right:** "The best for men's jewelry by their shape and power when you've got it on your finger." Rings, gothic crosses and stars, winged vanitas skull, heavy weight silver, Chrome Hearts, 2012.

Left: "These rings are important to me, especially the one with St. Martin which reminds me of St. Martin's church in Limoux where I went often as a child on Thursday afternoons." Foreground: ring reappropriating the Nazi Iron Cross by substituting the swastika with a pentagram, enameled metal, Alchemy, 2000; claw ring (ibid. p. 244) Background: fleur-de-lis ring, silver; silver ring depicting St. Martin; Tuareg ring, heart decorated with stylized motifs, silver. **Right:** From the Exorcist to the Arthur Legends, a mysterious imaginary... Diagonally from top to bottom: rings, opening coffin, chest, skull held like prey in claws, silver-plated metal and enamel, synthetic diamond, Alchemy Gothic and Carta Angleterre. Upper right: biker ring, hooded skull, silver and gilded bronze, circa 1970. Lower left: helm ring, articulated, silver and stone.

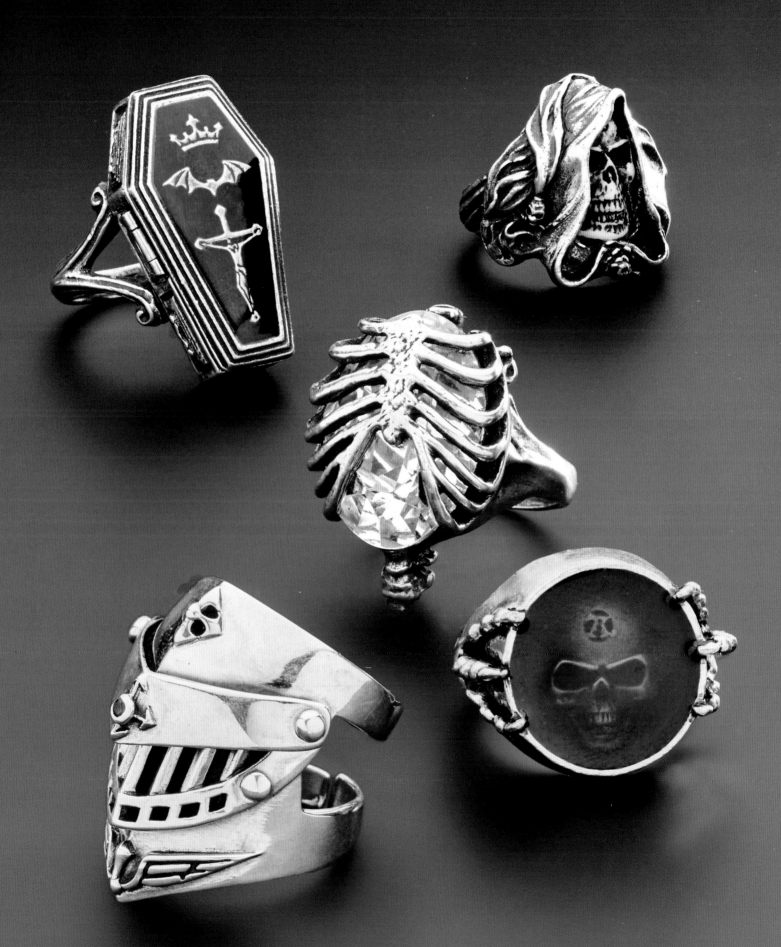

Left: The hand of God. American football champion's ring, enameled metal and rhinestones. **Right:** Dandy. The extrovert's ring, neoclassical foliate scroll pattern crowning the bezel, oval cut amethyst, yellow gold, 1940s. Signet ring, openwork initials "MV", floral motif on the shoulder, yellow gold, circa 1910–1920. "It was such a pleasure to find this one because it bears my children's initials, Mathilde and Victor."

3

GOTHIC

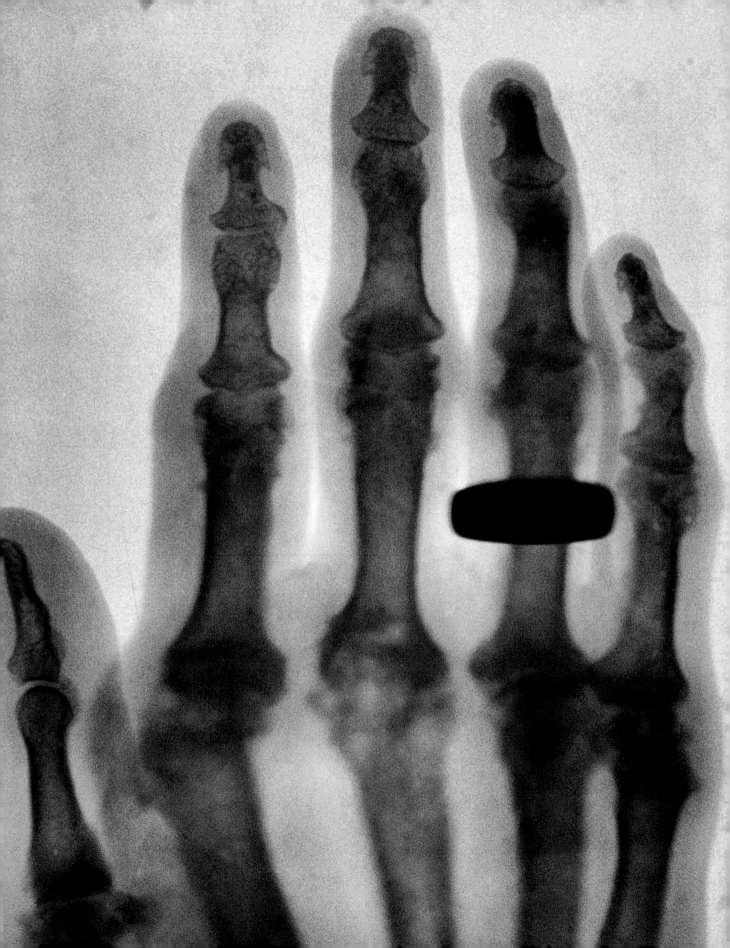

The gothic renaissance was born in Romantic England at the end of the 18th century and spread throughout Europe during the first half of the 19th century. A reaction to classicism, this architectural style included the great medieval religious and civil structures like the Basilica of Saint Denis, the Cologne cathedral, and Windsor Castle. The architects constructed edifices in a neoclassical taste, by highlighting their ancient decorations. Theoreticians like Augustus Pugin re-introduced certain arts like illumination and stained-glass windows, while jewelers rediscovered techniques like embossing, niello, and enamels. "They translated literature into metalwork and embossing, creating a 'feudal paraphernalia'," writes Henri Vever, as cited in "Le Bijou néogothique parisien" (The Parisian Neo-Gothic Jewel) by Jacqueline Viruega.

Indeed, writers like the Englishman Horace Walpole, author of *The Castle of Otranto*, and Victor Hugo with *The Hunchback of Notre Dame* were inspired by and participated in the distribution of this Medieval craze. The gothic novel, a literary movement of fantasy, used the architecture as a favored décor for the plots of its novels. Haunted castles, cemeteries, and the crypts of monasteries (p. 262) became the theatre of a combat between good and evil, and featured protagonists struggling with individual and collective fears. Gothic buildings were treated like characters in their own right, intensifying the sublime macabre and the anguish of the characters.

Bram Stoker's 1897 epistolary novel popularized the vampire, creating a mythic figure for exploring the psychoanalytical questions of the genre. A complex personality, Dracula is one of the most adapted myths in literature and in film. From the expressionist *Nosferatu* by Murnau to Jarmusch's highly sensual *Only Lovers Left Alive*, along with Coppola's grandiose *Dracula*, Morticia in the Addams family, and Tim Burton's roles for Johnny Depp, the aesthetic universe of the vampire built on and further inspired the iconography of the contemporary gothic movement, in its eccentricity and its taste for the bizarre.

Founded in 1979, the English group Bauhaus recorded their first single, "Bela Lugosi's Dead", a direct reference to the actor who played Count Dracula in 1931. This song was re-played in 1983 in the scene that opened the film *The Hunger* with Catherine Deneuve and David Bowie as vampires. The song is considered the foundational title of gothic rock, a darker and more melancholy music compared to punk. From The Cure to Siouxsie, artists gave themselves a new look to compliment an austere scenography. In contrast to the optimistic and brightly colored fashion of the hippies and less rebellious then punk, goth fashion played with contrasts: black clothing and hair, extremely white skin highlighted further by smoky make-up. The audiences of these concerts also began to adopt this aesthetic, as can be seen in photos taken in the London nightclub The Batcave, a temple for the gothic, which opened in 1982. The movement developed in England and in the United States, then in Germany with the emblematic group Das Ich, a duo with a demoniacal look. Since the 1990s, the controversial American singer Marilyn Manson has contributed to spreading goth culture worldwide.

The gothic ring developed out of all these inspirations. Typically worked in silver, its motifs include the movement's successive inspirations. Alchemy jewelers was created in 1977 in Manchester and is a current leader in gothic jewelry. Its designs represented in Gastou's collection include rings decorated with tri-lobe friezes that feature gothic characters (p. 86) or frightening gargoyles (p. 73). The symbols are either religious or occult, like St. Peter's cross or a pentacle. Angels rub shoulders with bats and coffin lids are covered in roses (p. 76). Chrome Hearts designs, founded in 1988 in Los Angeles, were worn by the Sex Pistols and Cher. A family-owned business with a gothic typography, their success brought them to work with some of the greatest designers like Karl Lagerfeld and Rei Kawakubo. These pioneers of Haute Couture appropriated the static canons of the gothic style, playing with the contrast of black and white in their fashion shows. They were followed by Alexander McQueen in 2001 with a collection celebrating the pageantry of Victorian mourning and John Paul Gaultier who created a collection around gothic heroines in 2014, similar to Japan's gothic Lolitas.

The gothic has maintained its counter-culture position over time, showcasing the uniqueness of the individual and a taste for the supernatural. A bona fide fashion of the 19th century, the style reappeared in the underground milieu of the 1980s before being launched into the world of fashion. As a music and film lover, as an aesthete and always attentive to trends, Yves Gastou retraces this gothic aesthetic in his men's rings.

Harold Mollet

Left: A beautiful little face to be wary of, because it can pierce you... Detail, angel ring, Lydia Courteille. **Right:** In the dish, two angel rings, white gold and rhodium-plated black, diamond paving on the sword and the eyes, Lydia Courteille, circa 2008. Top: flame ring, open work silver, 1980s.

Left: Wolf's Eye. Collection of vanitas skull rings: skeleton dance; skulls facing opposite directions, Abraxas; skull in flames: wolf's eye, metal and glass, Alchemy Gothic; winged skull; vanitas skull with a headache. **Right:** Rings out of a medieval dream. Gothic rings, left: silver-plated metal, garnet and amethyst; right: the Cross of Lorraine in enamel, marble in mother-of-pearl glass, metal, Alchemy Gothic, 1991 and 2005.

Left: Dream rings... Carry your cross and angel wings, Crystal Evolution. **Right:** *Edward Scissorhands*, gothic version. Articulated armor rings, silver, 1970s.

Left: "A knight's costume jewelry!" Gothic rings, crown decorated with skulls, rings set with synthetic gemstones, half-man half-dragon gargoyle character, bat, glass eye, Alchemy Gothic, 1997 to 2009. **Right:** "Would the devil have worn it?" Detail of the magnificent gothic ring of a gargoyle, plastic spikes coming out of the mouth, forehead and chin.

Peter Marino, architect, wearing his rings.

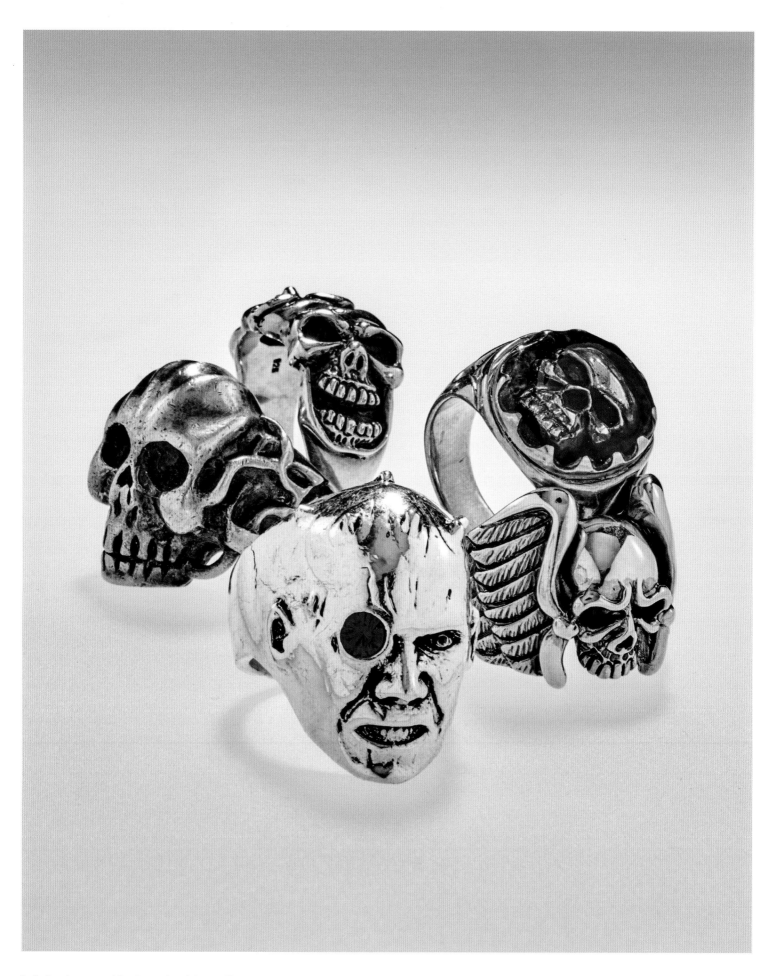

Left: Death pays a visit... Exceptional ring, coffin with ornate floral decoration, one-of-a-kind, silver, 1970s. **Right:** War wounds and collateral damage. Four vanitas skull rings, silver, enamel, Gemmex (left), Crystal Evolution (right). Foreground, avatar ring of Colonel Saul Tight, character from the television series *Battlestar Galactica*, silver and rhinestones, Crystal Evolution.

Left: "Rings to wear at Venice Carnival." Collection of flamboyant gothic rings, from left to right: stylized cross ring with foliate scroll pattern, square amethyst in the center, moving bell with sound on the inside; neo-renaissance ring, pearl and skull tassel, Alchemy Gothic, 2009; rectangular amethyst ring in silver, engraved with "god" and "roman order" on the band; skull ring, decorated with enameled pentagram, Alchemy Gothic, 2005. **Right:** Cathedral Era. Neogothic rings, from top to bottom and left to right: ring with stone held by claws, bat on the shoulder; clerestory ring; heart and bat-wing ring; effigy ring, bat ring, metal, enamel, synthetic gemstones, Alchemy Gothic and Carta, 1996 to 2005.

Left: Homage to Goethe's German Romanticism and Grimm's Fairytales. Neogothic, vanitas skull and bestiary rings, silver, Chris Stenzhorn, Rebeligion, 2015.
Right: Christ on the cross ring, one-of-a-kind, André Lassen, 2008. Ring in blackened silver, quotation from Bil Keane, famous comic book writer, engraved around the bezel: "Yesterday is history. Tomorrow is a mystery. Today is a gift of God.", Franz Marfurt Lucerne, L'Éclaireur. Foreground, medusa head ring.

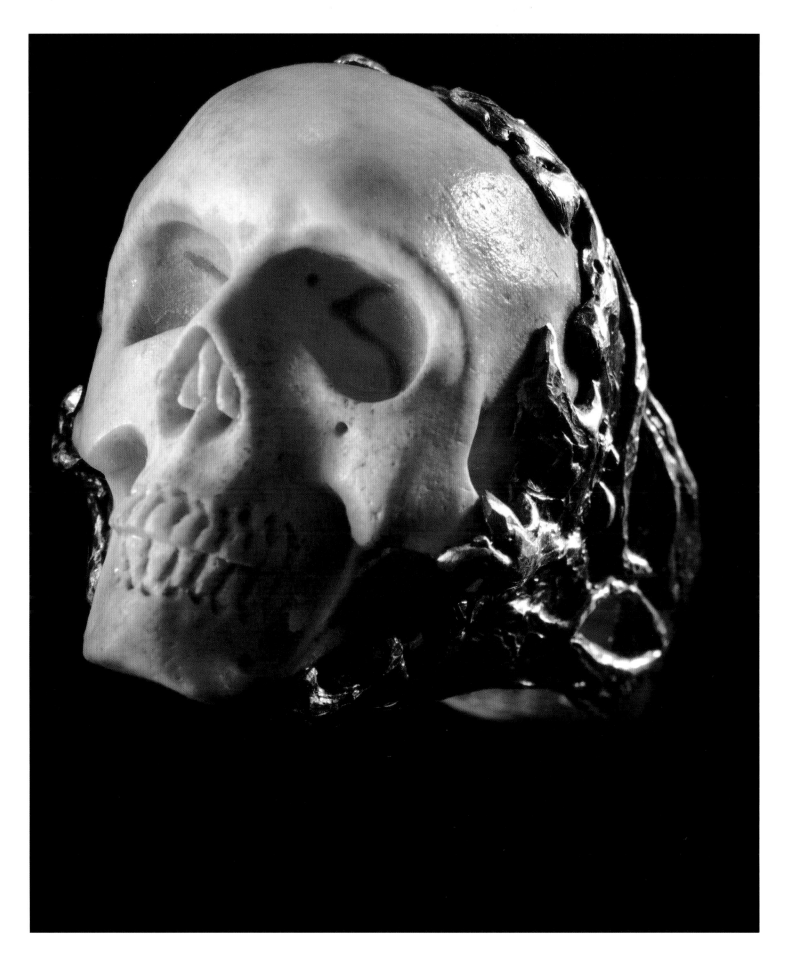

Left: Nosferatu. Foreground: ring, cross with four skulls, bone, 1970s. Background, from left to right: skull with transparent skullcap, set onto a silver ring, semi-precious gemstones set into the eye sockets, 1950–1960. One of Yves Gastou's favorite pieces, which he describes as an "artistic masterpiece." Vanitas skull ring, carved ivory, inner ring in yellow gold, Marc Gassier, 2011. **Right:** "Vrooom... vroom... I see the guy wearing this on his motorcycle... Fabulous!" Vanitas skull ring, ceramic skull surrounded by the flames of hell creating the bezel in solid silver, one-of-a-kind, 1970s.

Left: Good genie. Articulated ring, silver, circa 1970, detail reminiscent of the character of the genie from Aladdin's lamp. **Right:** Demonic mask. Ring with a Japanese demon as made famous in Noh theatre, silver, circa 1970.

Left: Celebrating the gothic: homage to Viollet-le-Duc. Vanitas skull rings, gothic calligraphy, poly-lobe cruciform friezes, silver-plated metal and enamel, Alchemy Gothic and Carta, 2000 to 2007. **Right:** "Men's rings but which take some daring to wear as a boy." Foreground: two hippie chic rings, baguette cut synthetic gemstone, poured metal bezel, Alchemy Carta, 2008; free form silver set with mandarin garnets, circa 1970. Background: Art nouveau revival ring featuring a dragonfly-woman, silver, La Mandragore; ring to hide poison or drugs, black stone held with claws, bat on the shoulder, Alchemy Gothic, 2002.

Left: "I love Jesus hearts, ghosts, and pirates." Iron Maiden rings, anonymous, 1970s, and Desperate Love heart, Corpus Christi. Heart of Jesus with a cross, silver and amethyst, Marc Gassier. Rings with the Virgin and the Languedoc cross, Corpus Christi. Open casket ring, United States, 1980s. **Right:** Infernal spiral. Clockwise: silver and metal rings with dragon wings, Ganesh (Indian craftsmanship), skeleton carrying a coffin with a cross (Alchemy Gothic, 2007), a winged fleur-de-lis, the grim reaper, a monstrous snake (Abraxas). Center: Portcullis signet ring, silver.

Left: "Perfection." *Fellow* ring, skulls, silver, diamond tears, M.A.R.S, Japan, 2004. Coffin ring, metal and rhinestone, Gemmex. Two-finger cross ring, surgical steel, Thomas V, 2013. **Right:** At knifepoint. Left from comb-knife: bishop's rings, openwork cross and ebony inlay, silver, 1970s. Right, from top to bottom: silver rings, cross pattée, vanitas skull with crown; ring in the shape of a crown with fleur-de-lis, Abraxas.

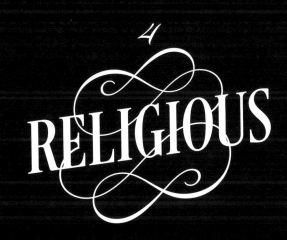

Louis XI converting/swearing allegiance to Christianity.

As successor to the first apostles, a bishop receives the emblems of his Episcopal responsibility from the ordaining prelate. The miter, his liturgical headdress, is knotted with two dewlaps symbolizing the Old and New testament. The crosier, also called the bishop's staff, is evocative of the shepherd guiding his flock. The pectoral cross (p. 104) completes his religious vestments and is a direct symbol of Christ's crucifixion. The final pontifical adornment is the Episcopal ring, worn on the fourth finger of the right hand. In use since the fourth century, this element of Episcopal finery is presented here in all its majesty. "Receive this ring as a seal of faith," are the words pronounced as the ring is given, endowing the jewel with a profoundly spiritual element. It is a sign of the priest's mystical union and faithfulness to the church and a reflection of the history of Christianity. The apostolic fathers wore simple rings marked with early Christian symbols like the Chi Ro and the fish. Ancient theologians like Tertullian and Clement of Alexandria forbade all profane and mythological representations. The Church became more established with the emperor Constantine's conversion to Christianity and its symbols became more evocative: the cross and the crucifixion nails, doves, St. Peter's keys, the *Agnus Dei*, and the rooster.

In the 17th century, Isadore of Seville, considered one of the Fathers of the Church, decreed that the ring must be made of solid gold and set with an unengraved precious stone. The rings began to feature cabochons of agate, citrine, crystal, garnet, and ruby. The amethyst, which was believed to ward off bad thoughts and protect from evil, became the bishop's stone. In his 1846 Archeological Annals, Adolphe Napoléon Didron poetically described *the* stone: "By combining the most pleasing nuances—purple, pink, and crimson—the amethyst echoes the humility of children, the fearful modesty of virgins, and Christian largesse, which, as its Latin name expresses, is a sacrifice of the self pushed to the peak of martyrdom. The amethyst represented Zebulon, ancestor of several apostles, and the peerlessly humble Saint Matthew." The splendor of the settings developed as the church grew richer over the centuries, until even relics of would-be martyrs in 17th century Eastern Europe were adorned, as shown in the photographic work of the art historian Paul Koudounaris in *Heavenly Bodies*.

However, these seals of piety and signs of heavenly protection were only reserved for the most important pontifical prelates, as Maximin Deloche explained in 1896, "The simple priests or clergymen, contrary to the miter-clad bishops and abbots, never had the ring

because, according to the terms of an old ecclesiastical order, they were not spouses of the Church like the bishops, they were its friends and lieutenants." Bishop's rings were delicately embossed and engraved with Christian iconography. Cherubs, St. Luke's winged bull, St. Mark's lion and the dove of the Holy Spirit rubbed shoulders with the Sacred Heart, grains of wheat and the tri-lobed cross. Cardinals bore the coat of arms of the Pope who promoted them, while the Pope wore a fisherman's ring with an image on the bezel of St. Peter fishing in his boat. Worn in service as well as in town, the rings were adjustable so they could be worn over gloves during mass and other processions.

These reproductions, masterpieces of the 19th century, also represent artisan know-how. The jeweler Froment-Meurice created a gold band (p. 103) to hold St. Peter's profile in enamel by Alfred Meyer, a ceramicist-painter of the Sèvres Manufacture. Engravers created pious cameos like this two-faced piece (p. 118/119) of the Virgin and Christ. Stoneworkers selected fine pearls (p. 102) and diamonds (p. 105) to kiss the reigning amethyst.

With the renewal of sacred art brought about by Father Couturier after the Second World War and the contemporary church architecture of the 1950s, the artists of the 20th century delivered simplified and geometric settings (p. 112) to echo this formal renewal. Cardinal Jean-Marie Lustiger followed by calling up modern sculptors like Jean Touret to create liturgical objects and decorations. The Ecumenical Vatican II Council, from 1962 to 1965, caused a rupture in the realm of religious jewelry. Under Pope Paul VI, the council fathers agreed to give up their traditional ring in exchange for a simple band. Drawn by Enrico Montini, the "sculptor to the Popes", the ring featured the crucified Christ, and the apostles Peter and Paul. With this return to basics, the contemporary Church and most recently in the stance of Pope Francis, the ring again enjoys a more pared-down style similar to the first Christians with their naked cross (p. 114) that can be easily imagined on the hands of a blue-collar priest.

Worn as jewelry or conserved as relics, antique episcopal rings have now become prized objects, sought out for their beauty and delicacy by collectors around the world, both men and women, believers or agnostics. Yves Gastou admits that it took patience to bring together the most exceptional pieces in his collection.

Harold Mollet

Left: "Exceptional bishop's ring: birth of the divine child, less heavy than rings with pearls or precious stones, and which heralds Pope Francis." Nativity ring, silver, embossed Latin inscription inside the band, 1950s–1960s. **Right:** Gold and myrrh to celebrate the birth of the Messiah. Exceptional bishop's ring, large amethyst encircled by a frieze of half-pearls, shield-shaped shoulder with specific designs in saltire on each, two keys on one (symbol of St. Peter granting access to heaven) and three roses with a sun on the other (symbol of Papal authority), 1900–1920.

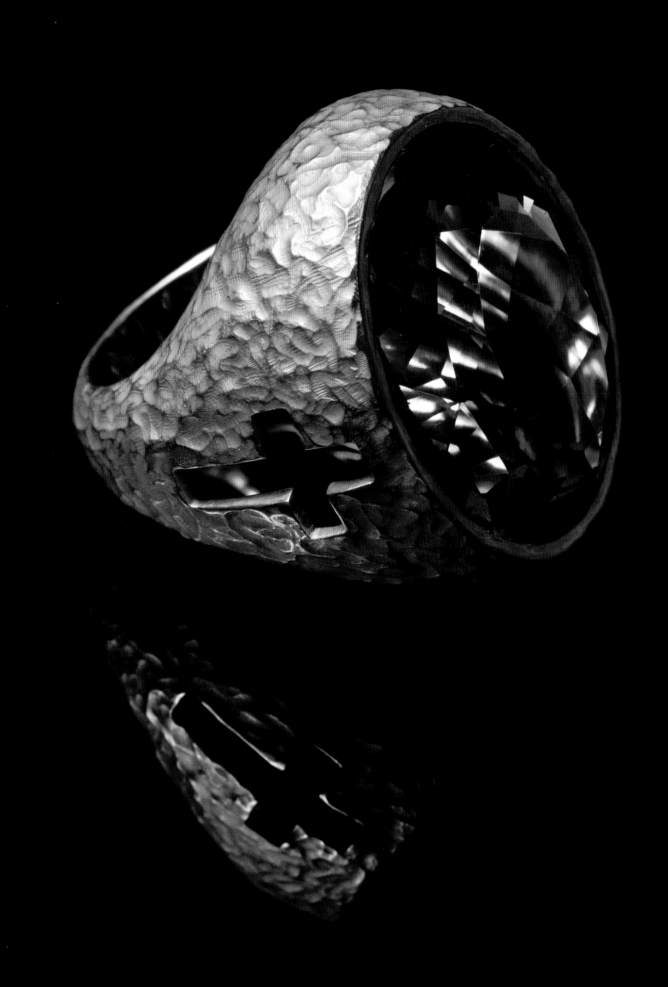

Left: "The diocese modernizes. Because of Vatican II." Episcopal ring, hammered openwork gold, amethyst, circa 1960. **Right:** Shadow and Light. "Priest's rings and black mass rings for satanic rituals..." Priest's rings from top to bottom: antique cross in copper; *Agnus Dei*; cameo with Templar cross pattée set in yellow gold (right); sorcery ring (lower right), stone embedded beneath a cage-shaped bezel, silver.

Left: "Other examples of rings that belonged to more serious bishops, those with simpler tastes, or maybe who didn't have patrons to buy them a more ornate ring." Episcopal ring, silver, vermeil, bronze, amethyst, citrine and garnet, Languedoc cross and Medieval era apostle's head. **Right:** "This is one of the rings that fits me like a glove. A very sensual ring, and also because it's Christ with his crown of thorns…" Ring, The Suffering Christ, silver, La Mandragore, ibid. p. 56–57.

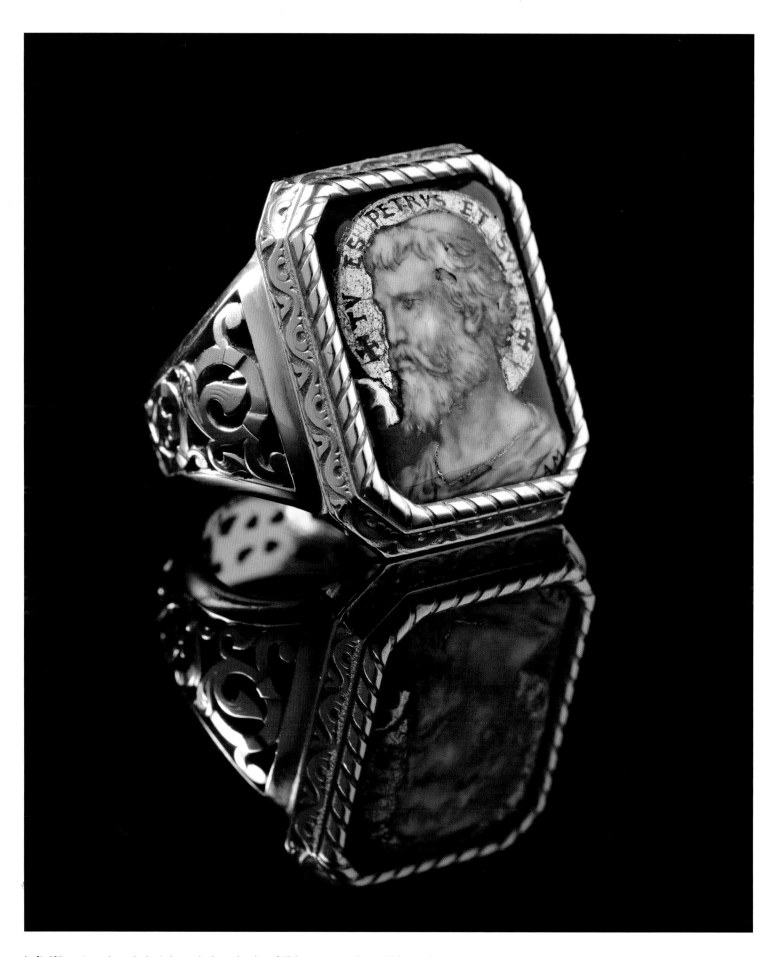

Left: 19th century rings designed to suit the splendor of 18th century prelates. Bishop's rings, embossed gold, pearls, amethyst, circa 1850 (foreground), citrine, cross engraved on the shoulder, circa 1880. **Right:** "Probably one of my most beautiful religious rings." Bishop's or Cardinal's ring, miniature of St. Peter painted on enamel by Alfred Meyer (known for having rediscovered the Limoges enamel technique), openwork embossed yellow gold, François-Désir Froment-Meurice with "FM" stamp dated 1866. Inscribed with the following: "Tu es Petrus et Super," ("And so I tell you Peter, you are a rock") extract from the *Gospel according to St. Matthew*, Chapter 16, Verse 18, in which Jesus Christ grants governance of the church to the apostle Peter.

Left: "The complete set! But I never dared wear them together." Episcopal finery, cross set with baguette cut amethysts, decorated with palm-fronds at the extremities; octagonal cut amethyst ring, pearls encircling the bezel, yellow gold, 1850–1880. **Right:** "Extremely high-quality, elegant jewels." Bishop's ring, oval cut amethyst, encircled with diamonds, cross on the shoulder, circa 1880. Ring with moving parts, adjustable so the bishop can wear it with or without gloves, acanthus leaf on the shoulder, orange opal cabochon, Charles X era (1820–1830).

Left: "Two rings to display one's faith. The one with the Christ is a rare Spanish model. It was worn by a devout nobleman or an upper bourgeois." Ring with the Suffering Christ, band in embossed scales to represent the fish of the early Christians, guilloché gold, Spain, 1900–1930. Holy Spirit dove ring, guilloché gold, Malta, 1900–1930s. **Right:** Detail.

Left: "The decorative work and engraving makes this an exceptional bishop's ring, worthy of the greatest jewelers." Ring, close set aquamarine, cross on the shoulder, yellow gold, 19th century. **Right:** "What makes this ring special is that it could have been worn for ceremonial purposes as well as during the day." Episcopal ring, yellow gold and amethyst, decorated with vine leaves and flowers on a matte background, sunflower on the shoulder, symbol of immortality, first half of the 20th century.

Left: Thou shall not kill. Curio ring, coming from André Breton's collection and shaped like a church. Christ on the cross on the exterior, small characters and a crucifix in relief on the interior. German craftsmanship, probably inspired by Jewish house-shaped wedding rings, vermeil, signed "Bos" on the verso, 19th century.
Right: "Beautiful examples of 19th century prelate rings. The engravings are magnificent. All the great jewelers were competing in terms of dexterity and creativity to satisfy their bishop clients." Lower left: Episcopal band from Monseigneur Taurin-Cahagne, missionary in Ethiopia, died in 1899, filigree and granulated yellow gold, oval amethyst, palm-frond on the shoulder. Center: bishop's ring, yellow gold, openwork palm motif on the shoulder (symbol of the Christian martyrs), rectangular amethyst, 19th century. Right: bishop's ring, filigree, granulated, and highlighted yellow gold, cherub in ronde-bosse on the shoulder, oval citrine, 19th century.

Left: "This 1950s ring has exceptional architecture, both imposing and powerful." Cruciform bishop's ring, amethyst, sigil symbol on the bezel, face-to-face ewes on the shoulder, 1950s. **Right:** "The band on this ring makes it incredible, the prowess of the design! It's one of my favorites." Bishop's rings, cruciform paving on the bezel around the central sapphire, amethyst encircled with diamonds, St. Lawrence's gridiron in flames on the left shoulder and a thorned heart of Jesus, 1900–1930.

Left: Fraternal Church vs the Flamboyant Church. "This ring with its cross rising from the ashes like a reminder of the early Christians illustrates the battle between the powerful church with its spectacular jewels, and the modern church of Father Couturier, with its dry stone architecture and glass paving stones on concrete by Corbusier." Bishop's ring, silver, cross in relief, 1960s. **Right:** Exceptional nobleman-cum-archbishop or cardinal ring, shield of arms topped with a ducal crown, band embossed with grapes and flowers, set with pear cut amethysts, yellow gold, 19th century.

Left: "It took me some time to find this one. I love angels." Episcopal ceremonial ring, winged angels on the shoulder, smoky quartz encircled with rose cut gemstones, yellow gold, second half of the 19th century. **Right:** "These three rings are from Mellerio dits Meller, the oldest jeweler at the place de Paris and the most important supplier for clergy of the 18th century. They're a reflection of an era when bishops wore true works of art, masterpieces of design." Episcopal rings, yellow gold, line of pearls or rope around the stone (citrine and amethyst), Mellerio dits Meller, 19th century. The model with the shaft of wheat on the shoulder, a symbol of transubstantiation, was created for the Archbishop of Rouen, Monseigneur Edmond Frédéric Fuzet (1839–1915). It bears the inscription: "Notre-Dame de Grâce" (Our Lady of Grace), and is dated June 19, 1913, date of enthronement.

"When I wear this ring, I can choose between the Holy Virgin and Christ." Two-sided ring, carnelian cameo, yellow gold, 19th century.

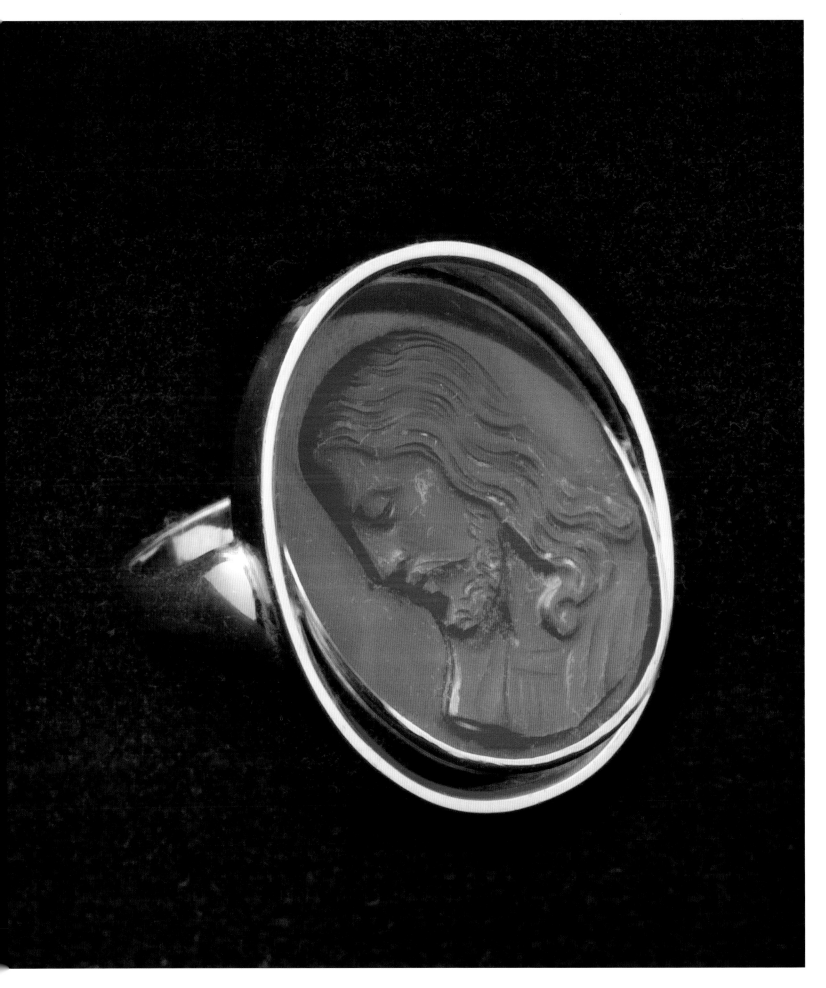

Left: "I've always been interested in these rings because they are extremely feminine. They make me think of Fellini films with transvestite priests." Episcopal rings, yellow gold, octagonal cut amethyst and openwork cross on the shoulder, pink topaz encircled with diamonds, embossed cross frieze on the band, 19th century. **Right:** "Bishop's rings for the new generation, structured like the new concrete churches of the 1950s and 60s. They simultaneously underscore post-war ecclesiastical power." Left: ring of Monseigneur Gaston, bishop of Saint-Pierre de Chaillot in Paris's 15th arrondissement, yellow gold, shiny round cut amethyst set on a pyramidal bezel, martyr's wheel, sword and palm-frond on the shoulder, stamp of goldsmith Maurice Poussielgue-Rusand, dated 1903. The wheel and the sword are symbols of the martyrs St. Catherine and St. George of Lydda. Right: bishop's ring, octagon cut amethyst, cross on the shoulder and the bezel, yellow gold, circa 1950.

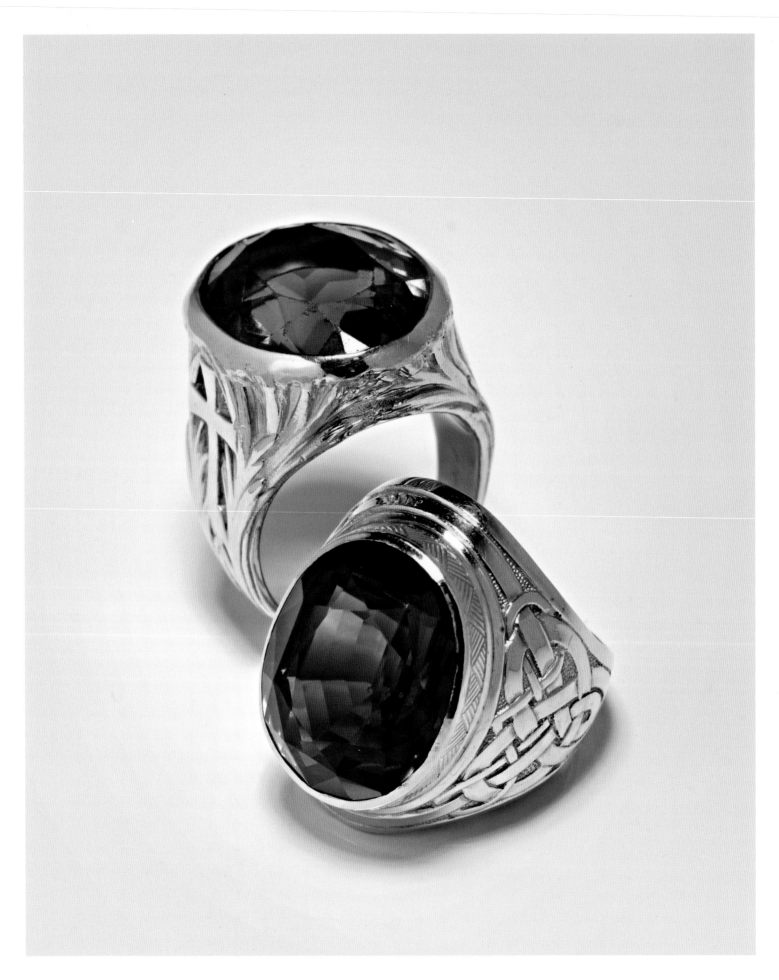

Left: The clergy follow fashion, which lightens as the church does after Vatican II, but without renouncing artistic quality. Two bishop's rings, oval close-set amethysts, cross on the shoulder for one, hand-embossed interlacing, yellow gold, 1950–1960. **Right:** Gemspring. Collection of bishop's rings, amethysts and citrines,

embossed gold, 19th century.

5

VANITAS
SKULLS

Vanitas skulls are a major theme in Gastou's collection. Situated somewhere between the moralizing "Memento Mori" and the hedonism of "Carpe Diem", Gastou celebrates the representations of life and death as depicted in both antique and contemporary jewelry.

Personifications of Death have fascinated humans forever. Every culture does this in a different way, either directly or through some figure charged with guiding souls to the underworld: the robed Grim Reaper with his scythe, Thanatos the son of Nyx, the angel Azrael shared by the Hebrew, Muslim, and Sikh traditions, the Aztec god Mictlantecuhtli, Yama in India, or the Shinigami of Japan. In the Christian tradition, the Four Horsemen of the Apocalypse initiate the end of the world and the Last Judgment. The final, dark-colored horse brings "Death" with him, as depicted by *St. John's Vision* by Gustave Doré. Art, whether sculpture or painting, music or literature, has used these emaciated faces and bare skulls as reminders of human mortality. Macabre art is a natural part of funeral architecture, featuring the deceased with a frightening realism, gathering skeletons in catacombs and ossuaries like the one in Sedlec in the Czech Republic with its majestically solemn chandelier. These collections, similar to the works of Dante or Virgil which illustrate the individual's journey toward death, can be found in the contemporary work of Marc Gassier (p. 173). His intricately entwined gold skeletons (p. 186) evoke the macabre dance that came out of France's Medieval mystery plays. Through a series of skits, Death carries off the living with no concern for social status. This visual representation of the idea of life's ephemeral nature can be traced across the centuries in frescoes and engravings. It was put to music by Camille Saint-Saens in 1874 in a captivating waltz, which was then, a hundred years later, re-made by Jacques Higelin in an extraordinary version called "Champagne." The frenzy with which artists have made their skeletons dance, in the vein of Rimbaud when he said, "La vie est la farce à mener par tous'" (Life is the farce which everyone has to perform) has always inspired film: *Le squelette joyeux* (The Happy Skeleton) by the

Lumière brothers, *le Cake-Walk Infernal* by Méliès and Walt Disney's *The Skeleton Dance* from the series *Silly Symphonies*. These carnivalesque masquerades were (and still are today) celebrated by the Venetian jeweler Codognato. From amongst his clients—Coco Chanel, Luchino Visconti, and the gallery owner Ileana Sonnabend—the discreet designer especially remembers Magritte: "He really understood the farcical, light side of the vanitas skull. He came to the shop in the 1960s to buy one for his wife. And he asked us to decorate the skull with a little bowler hat!"

As St. Matthew wrote, "Tomorrow looks after itself." Mexico, in particular, with its Day of the Dead, treats death with humor and facetiousness. Decorated with bright colors and flowers, the *calaveras* are a fusion of pre-Hispanic ritual and evangelical values which was mythologized by the nationalists in 1920. Gastou's collection includes many examples, like this embossed skull (p. 178) or this one in gold (p. 166) with its crazy look and Virgin medallion over the mouth. The most symbolic character of this festival is Catrina. A female skeleton dressed in European-style finery and wearing a large hat, she was popularized by Diego Riviera in a 1947 fresco and modernized in *The Book of Life* in 2014.

Damien Hirst took the decorative element of the *memento mori* to an extreme in 2007 with his sculpture "For the Love of God", covered with more than 8,600 diamonds. The work has become a reference, cited in the exhibition, *Vanitas. From Caravaggeio to Damien Hirst* at the Maillol Museum and in Elizabeth Quin's *Le Livre des vanités* (*The Book of Vanitas*) in 2010. The artist Christian Breul Von Maria reinterprets the theme with his two-faced skull (p. 195). The designer Crystal Evolution has an entire rhinestone-studded collection of skulls (p. 138), hearts (p. 172) and pirate iconography. A treasure for contemporary pirates to hoard in memory of marauders who once rode the open seas beneath their skull and crossbones flag. The symbol was appropriated by soldiers as well, including aviator Charles Nungesser who had it painted on his Nieuport 17 during the first world war.

A pair of bikers at the Motor Cycle and Cycle show in London, November 1960.

When death becomes increasingly tangible, humans create objects to fight back against the idea of oblivion. When faced with the loss of loved ones, elegies and funeral songs accompany mourning jewels (p. 37). Fashionable since the 16th century in England and in Europe, the "mourning" rings were engraved with the name of the deceased and sometimes contained a lock of hair and a portrait. When the horrors of war severely tested the men in the trenches, French soldiers sculpted rings from shrapnel and the rests of mortar shells (p. 252), "Parce que de matière à leur gré criminelle / L'homme efface au burin la tare originelle / Bijou dont le seul prix s'estime au sentiment[2]" (because men wield the chisel on the metal / Erasing its original wicked proposal / For a jewel appraised by sentiment alone).

After the end of the second world war, bodies marked in the style of Otto Dix and the tortured spirits of Francis Bacon revealed the cruelty of death. Veterans readapted to civil society as best they could. In California, members of the Marine Corps, Air Force, and Infantry turned to motorcycles, an activity "that could get their blood pumping once again," as William L. Dulaney wrote in *A Brief History of "Outlaw" Motorcycle Clubs*.

In 1947, *Life* magazine published a photograph by Barney Petersen showing a drunk motorcyclist during a biker gathering in Hollister. Hollywood followed in 1953 with the cult film, *The Wild One*. Marlon Brando on his Triumph as head of a gang that terrorized a small town. And so was born the myth of the rabble-rousing biker with his black leather jacket and rumbling exhaust pipe. Protest becomes a way of life. *Rebel Without a Cause* in 1955 defined this rebel youth and established James Dean as an icon of American counter-culture. He was also astride a Triumph. What followed were the violent biker gangs: Hells Angels, Bandidos, Mongols, considered the "1%" in contrast to other motorcycle enthusiasts. Smitten with their freedom and with mechanics, these bikers hit the road Jack Kerouac-style. In *Easy Rider*, Dennis Hopper crosses the US on a chopper with an enormous, stretched-out fork and stripped of all superfluous parts. The culture of customizing bikes was paralleled with the perfecto leather jacket with its shields, patches, and anti-establishment slogans. These same motifs were worn as rings (p. 192), helmeted skulls

adorned with fleur-de-lis, marked with the Malta cross and surrounded by flames like the Ghost Rider skull (p. 155), an incarnation of Faust from the Marvel Comics universe. Beginning in the 1970s, this biker aesthetic began to appear in the American market incarnating every character from the judge to the samurai, from the Indian chief to the pharaoh. Gastou assembles this entire universe in his collection, laid out in his ring trays in the style of his famously unexpected pairings, which reveal the power of these objects.

After having conquered the United States, the movement went international. In France, Edith Piaf sings her "Hymn" to the motorcycle before the first biker clubs appeared in Paris at the end of the 1960s. They gathered on the weekends on the Boulevard Saint-Germain at the Café Mabillon until a French chapter of the Hells Angels was established in 1981. Amsterdam's artisan blacksmith André Lassen, a fan of antique weaponry, transformed metal to create high-quality rings (p. 141) which are coveted by international celebrities like Richard O'Brien, director of the wacky *Rocky Horror Picture Show*, and Chris Stein, the guitarist from Blondie.

Much like the chess match in Bergman's *The Seventh Seal*, humans have always played a game with death. Gastou's game is to collect. "The rings have no beginning and no end. Despite how small they are, they can show us an entire universe on a small one or two-centimeter surface.[3]" The simplicity of vanitas skulls, like the designs by the Japanese jeweler M.A.R.S (p. 90 and 183), and their extreme purity (p. 137), help us remove some of death's obscurity.

Harold Mollet

---

1   *A Season in Hell*, 1873.
2   Poem by Francis Bergau, written in 1916, entitled "The Ring" with the epitaph, "from the trenches".
3   Quote from the exhibition *Small Size, Great Aesthetics—A Hundred and One Rings* at the Museum of Jewelry in Pforzheim, Germany, 2013.

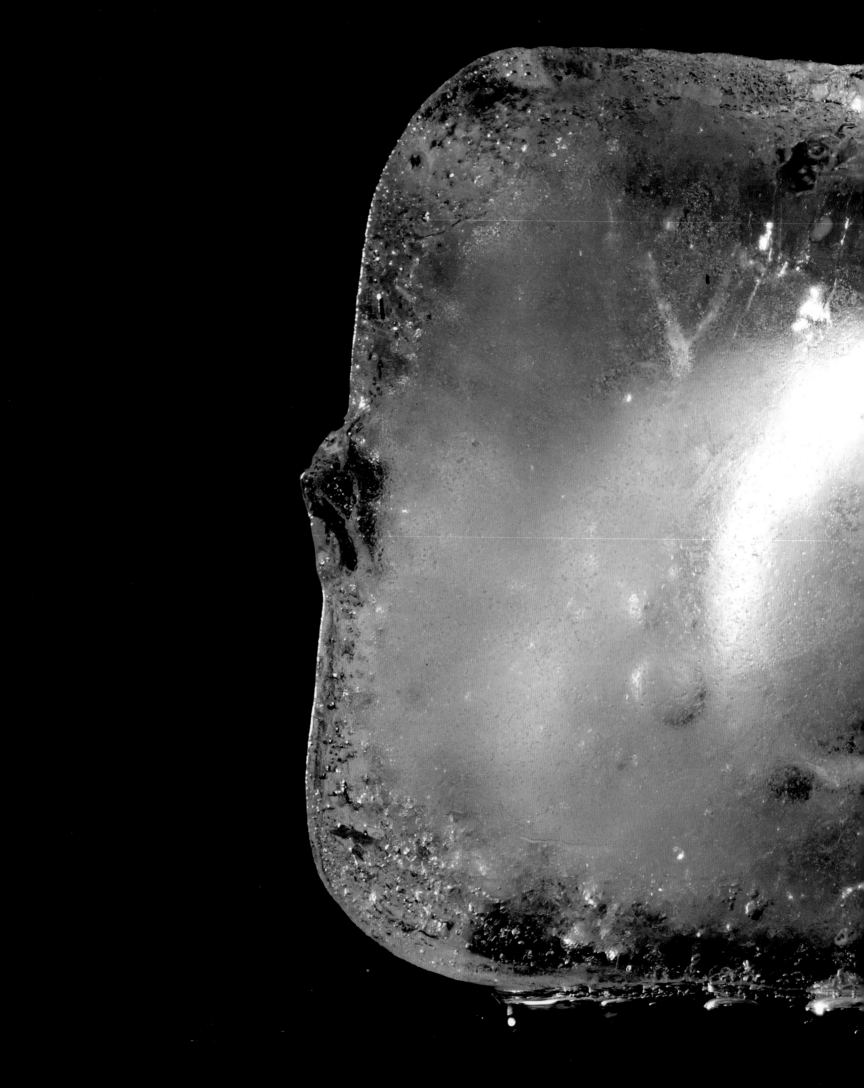

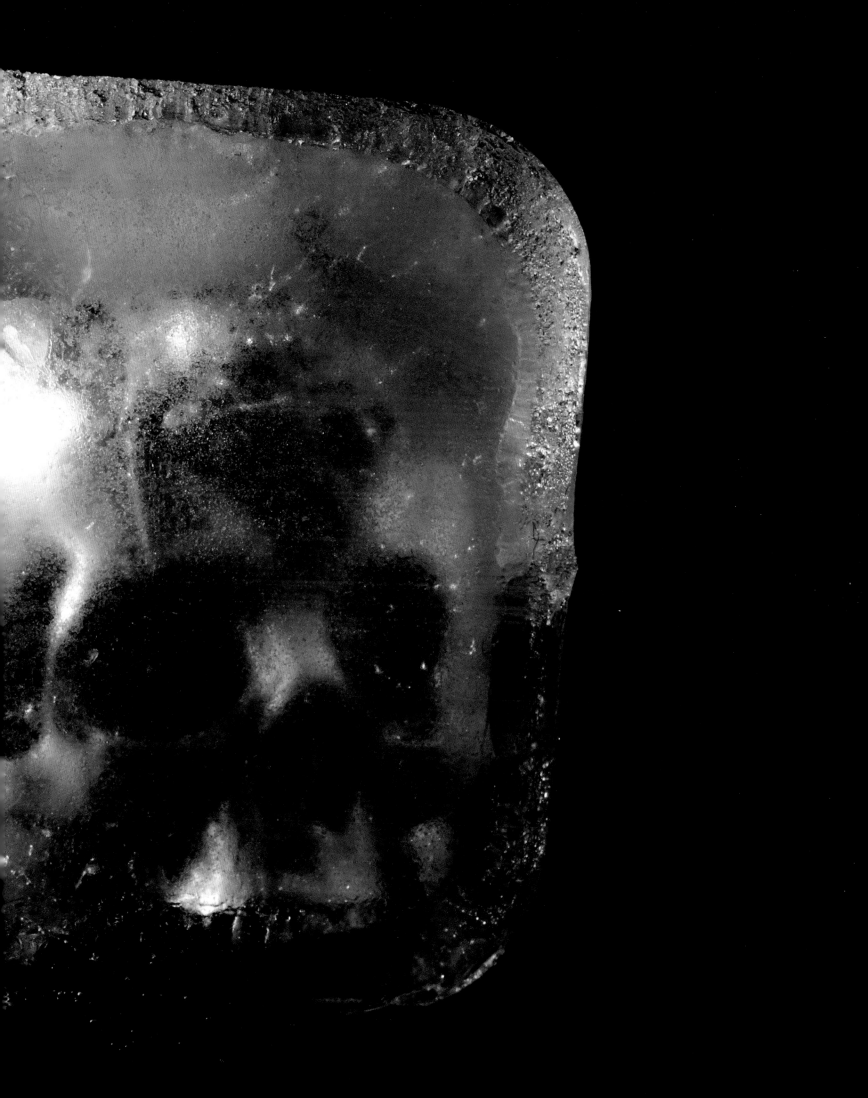

Left: "Flames rising up from the pavement; a ring straight out of *The Wild One*." **Right:** "The grim reaper in his long cape and funeral procession." Vanitas skull

rings, silver, bronze, ivory and crystal, circa 1970.

Left: Group of men's rings, 19ᵗʰ century to contemporary. Upper ring, a wink to the Incan mummy in *Tintin*, "the one who brings down the fire of heaven," in *The Seven Crystal Balls*, ibid. p. 154. **Right:** Why not red and the black together? Rings, silver and crystal.

Left: Christ and two thieves. Foreground: vanitas skull ring, band pressed into the jawbone, silver-plated metal, Alchemy Gothic. Background: vanitas skull in a turban, silver, Abraxas. **Right:** Vanitas skull ring set with rhinestones, ibid. p. 157.

Left: The altar of the dead. 19th century angel design holy water font, vanitas skull necklaces and rings, silver, vermeil and rhinestones. **Right:** Assortment of men's rings, 19th century to contemporary.

Left: "According to my mood, mask or vanitas..." Transformation rings, Crystal Evolution. **Right:** Assortment of vanitas rings, 1970s. Top, skull ring, Corpus Christi. 139

Left: "For a cabinet of curiosities." Large *Oeil du diable* (Devil's Eye) ring, solid silver, brilliant cut diamonds, rhodolite garnet cabochon on the top of the skull, one-of-a-kind, Alina Alamorean, 2012. **Right:** Vanitas skull ring, white gold, hematite, round brilliant cut, André Lassen, circa 1970.

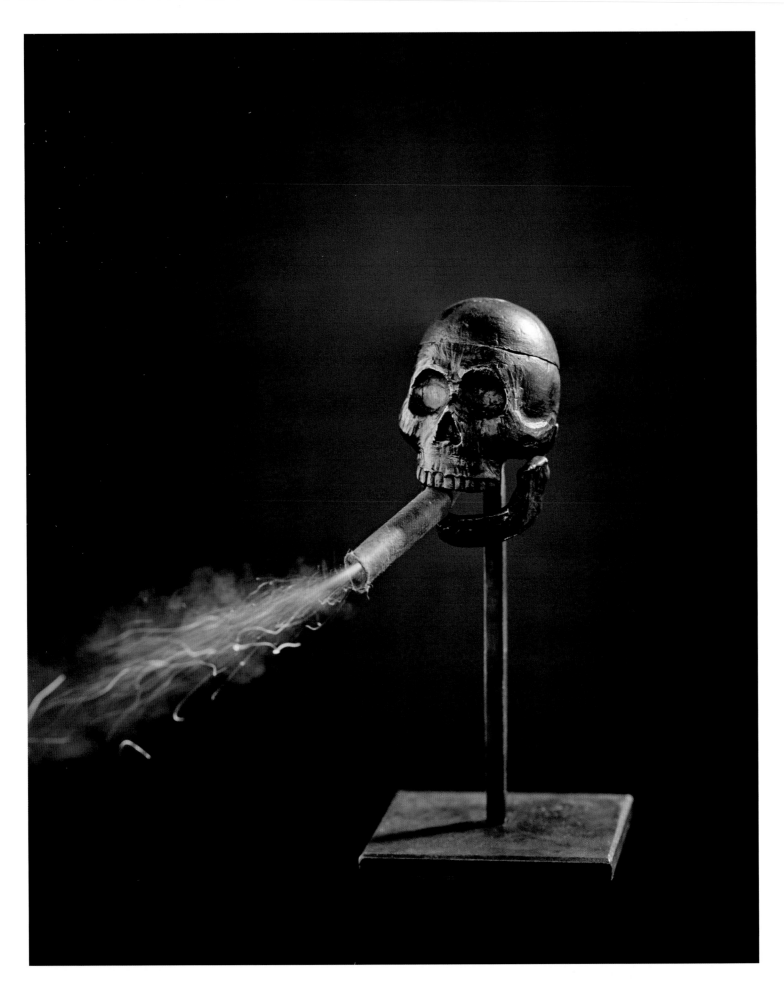

Left: "God smokes Havanas." Sculpture ring in three inserted and removable parts, bronze, one-of-a-kind, Lucien Miltin, 1921. **Right:** Detail of the sculpture-puzzle composed of the jawbone base, a vanitas skull ring, and finally the skullcap.

Left: Neo-renaissance rings very similar to those worn by Henri III's mignons. Baboon rings, darkened silver, yellow gold, Baroque pearl, mother-of-pearl cabochon, Grazia e Marica Vozza, 2007. **Right:** "These 1960s ring are a lovely illustration of the biker universe, Hells Angels and other hippies. The two holding hands also make me think of the large hands decorating the pillars of the Publicis Drugstore on Saint-Germain-des-Prés. Each time I go to Paris, I get off the train and go directly there. I love getting a drink and going down to the boutique. Many years later, I managed to buy one of the bronze pieces that had been distributed around after the demolition from the fantastic decorator Slavik." Foreground: vanitas skull rings, silver and gilded bronze, circa 1960. Background: ring with two hands holding, distressed metal, Alchemy Gothic, 2006.

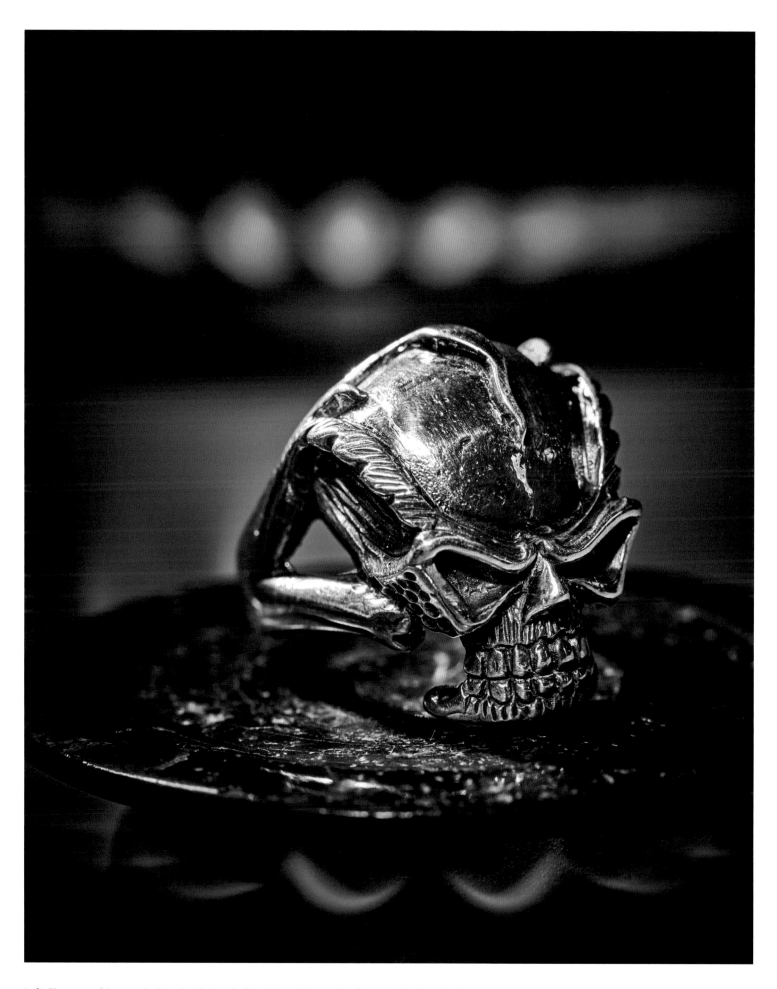

Left: The army of Sauron shadows in *The Lord of the Rings*. Helmeted and crowned vanitas skull rings, pewter, silver, and rhinestones, 1970s. **Right:** "You will burn in hell!" Vanitas skull rings, circa 1970.

Jean-Philippe Mollereau, called Aden, co-founder of Gavilane (men's jewelry designer) wearing his own designs of vanitas skull rings and bracelets made of antique components in ivory and wooden rosary beads. **Following double page spread:** G&S.

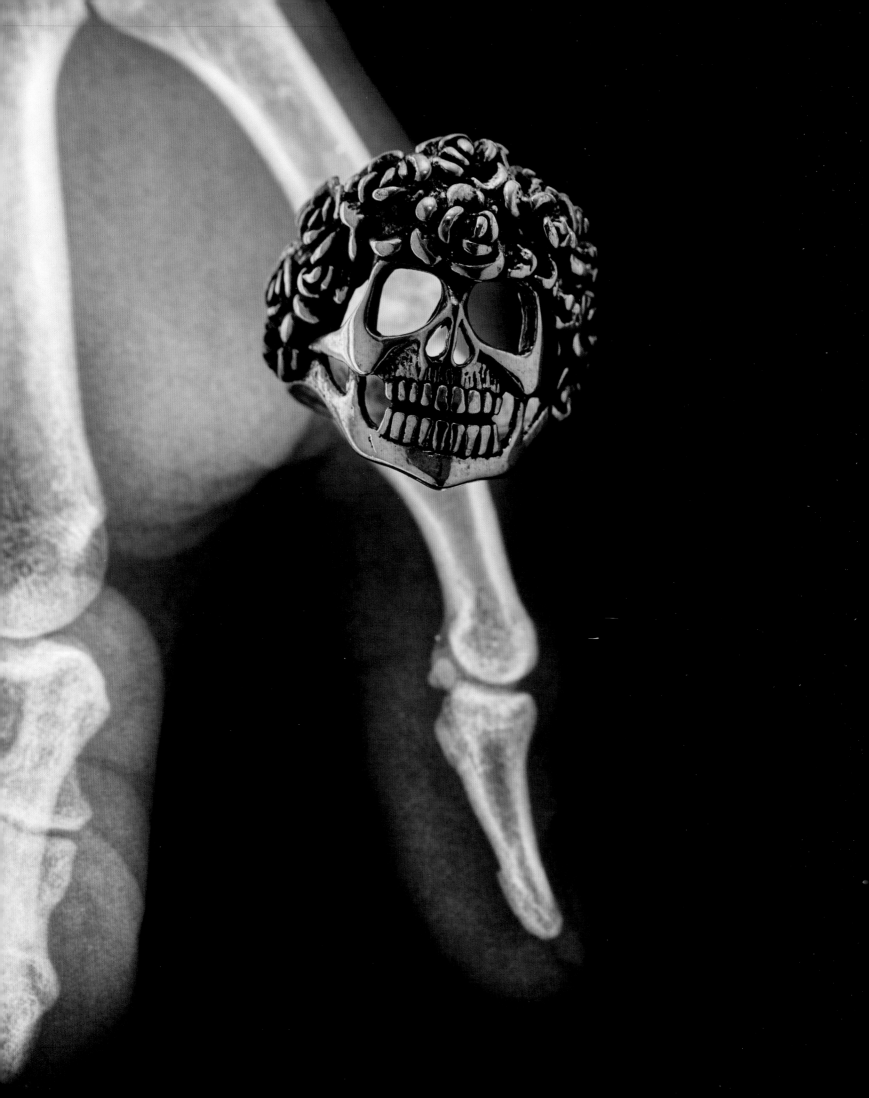

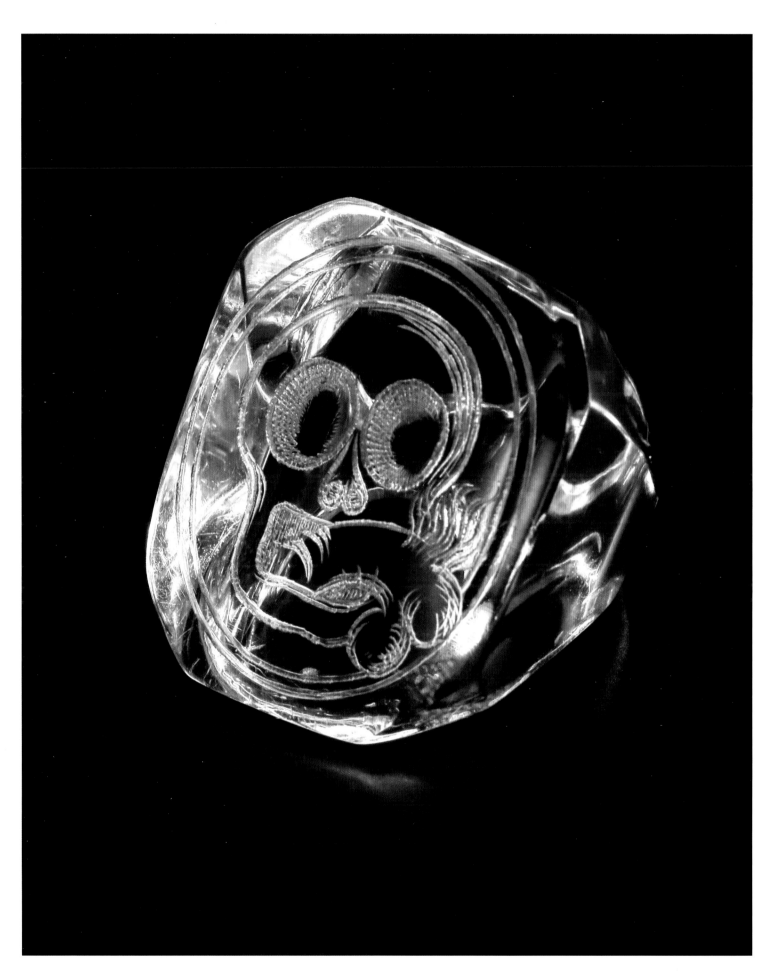

Left: Homage to Wim Delvoye: X-ray of human frailty; but rest assured this is a "controlled" death—inoffensive, funny, and gadgetized, covered with flowers or rhinestones, trendy accessory and iconic in our consumer society. Ring, flowered vanitas skull, 1970s. **Right:** "Beauty is everywhere, one just has to look." Suggestive. Erotic ring, engraved altuglas, one-of-a-kind, circa 1970.

Left: Left, two vanitas skull rings and coat-of-arms, silver, Mexico; Marie medallion ring, Corpus Christi; Foreground, Christ vanitas skull ring, 1970s; bullet on the white skull, Jacques Monory, silver, copper, 38 special bullet, Maeght edition, signed and numbered; ibid. p. 132. **Right:** "Whoever strays from the path of prudence comes to rest in the company of the dead." Bible quotation. From top to bottom, large vanitas skull rings in silver: Lucifer covering a king's skull with a shroud; flames rising from the sides of a skull with a sardonic smile, standing skeleton.

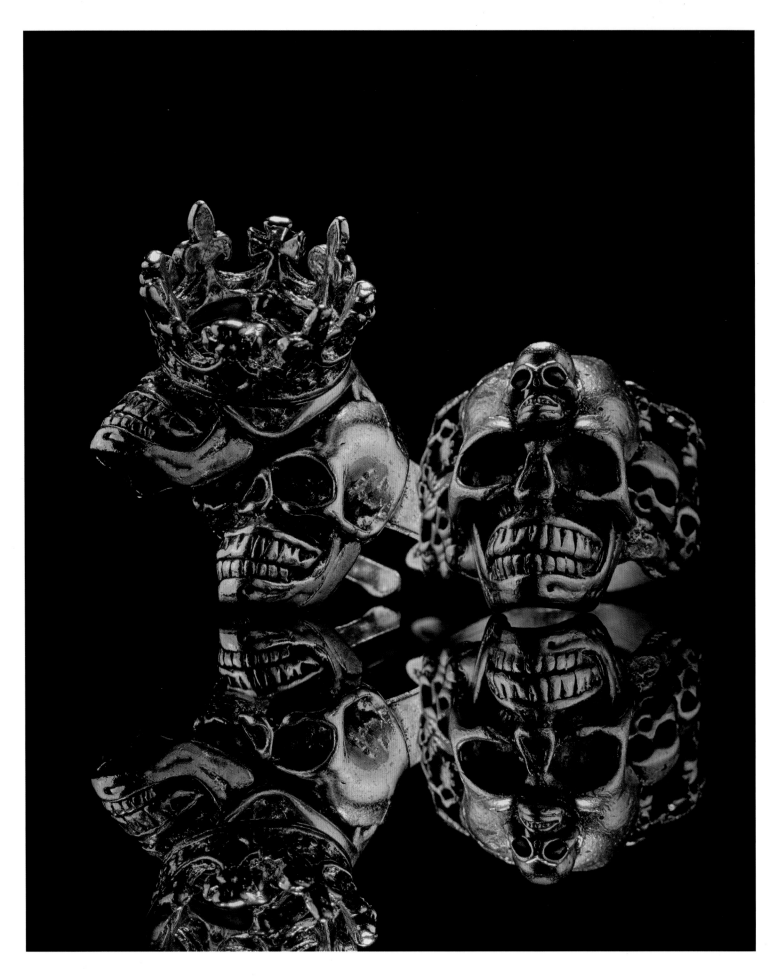

Left: Royal funeral. Vanitas skull rings, movable crown, silver-plated metal and rhinestone, Gavilane. **Right:** *Ghost Rider*. Vanitas skull rings on the fingers of a skeletal hand (belt buckle), from left to right: American rapper; polished silver skull, red glass over a skull; skull with facets, surgical steel, Thomas V. Lower left: vanitas skull covered with rhinestones, ibid, p. 134.

Left: Macabre trophy. Set into the eyesockets and the nose: vanitas skull rings, silver, 1970s. "The one with Guimard-style volutes is one of my favorite rings, because of its Art Nouveau feel, and the other with the Templars cross on the forehead which is about the knighthood—in other words, my two first loves." Set in the jaw: Samurai ring (left); claw ring holding a skull, Abraxas. **Right:** Iron mask. *Jason Zombie Skull and Doppler*, silver, 2 Saints. **Following double page spread:** Ring tray. Biker rings, silver-plated metal, United States, G&S.

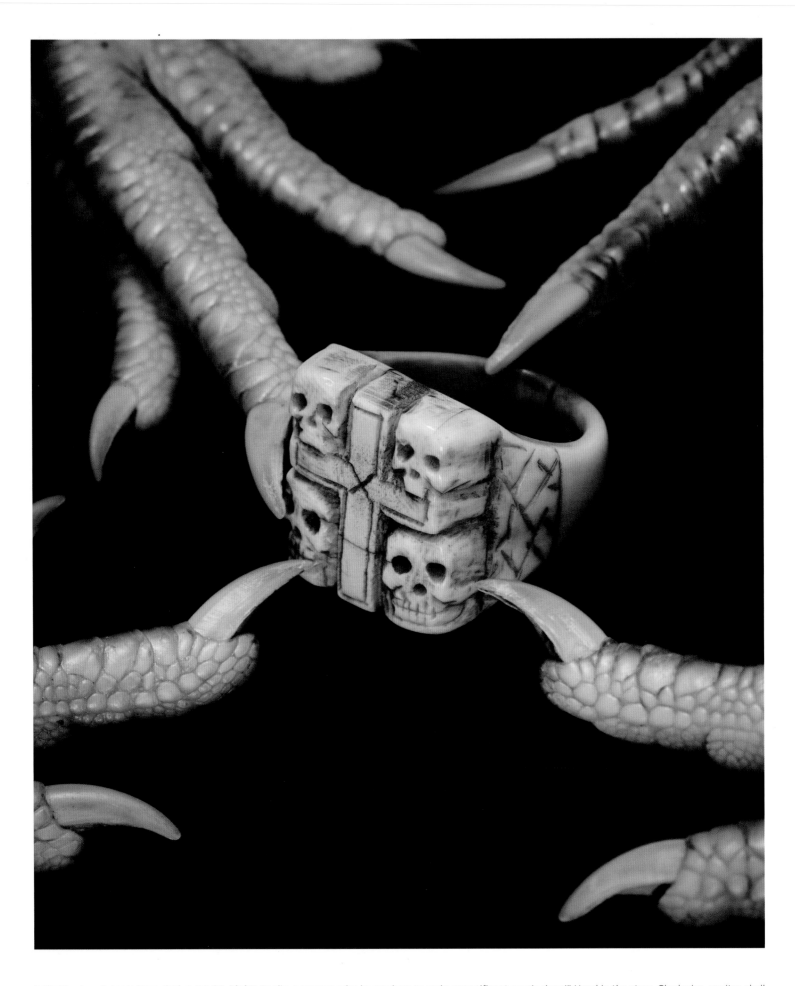

Left: Voodoo. Satanic Ring, ibid. p. 82-83. **Right:** "Lydia, a woman who knows how to make magnificent men's rings!" Head in the stars. Clockwise, vanitas skull rings: scarred skull, Lydia Courteille: forehead and eye sockets in rhinestones, Thomas Sabo: crown of thorns engraved on the top of the skull and amethyst-set cross covering the forehead, Lydia Courteille; skull with a starry eye-patch; steel skull by KoolKatana.

Left: Ex voto. Vanitas skull crowned with plants and fruits, Ugo Cacciatori, L'Éclaireur, Cameo rings, ibid, p. 30. Gothic cross signet ring, Rebeligion, ibid, p. 80. Cruciform ring, silver, Abraxas. **Right:** Two vanitas skull rings from the 20th century. Rings, silver, crystal, Crystal Evolution.

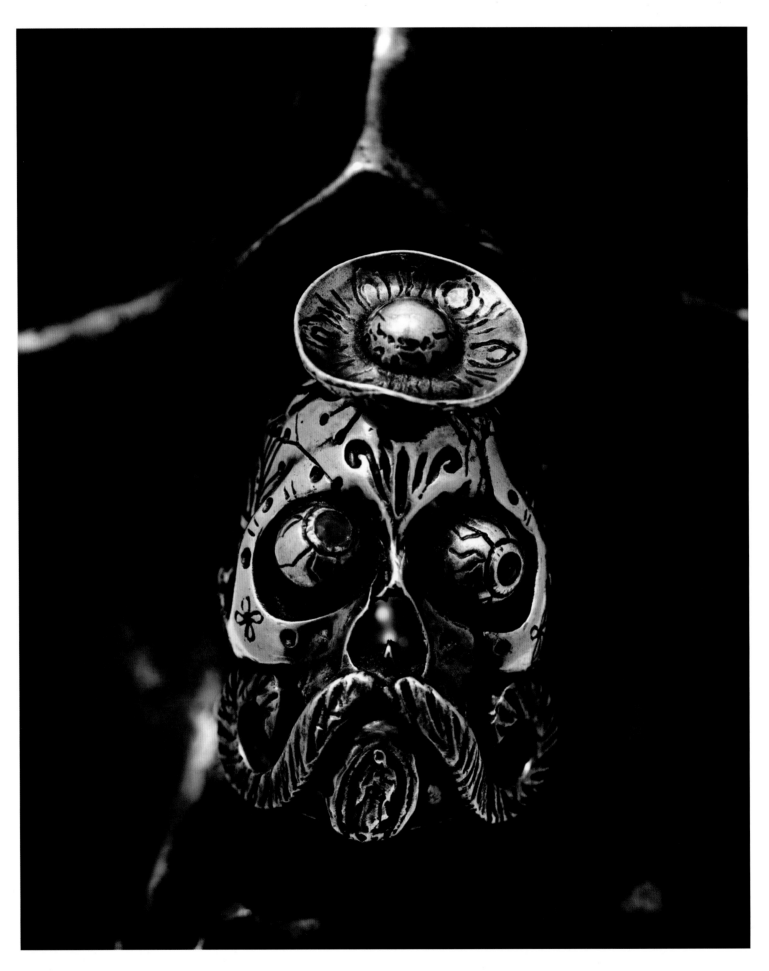

Left: "I love this one like crazy!" A ring to wear for the Day of the Dead, with the medallion of the Virgin Mary covering the man's beard. Detail of this exceptional Mexican ring, 1960s. **Right:** "A shocking ring, and one of my most beautiful rings." Screwed into the skull: vanitas skull ring, yellow gold, round brilliant cut black diamond set into the jaw, circa 1970, André Lassen.

Left: Rings: vanitas skull, scarab, Viking, silver, 1970s. **Right:** War, power, and hell. Assortment of vanitas skull rings in silver, 1970s. From top to bottom: SS helmet, a knight's helmet, princely crown, pirate hat and eyepatch, horns of Beelzebub.

Phantom of the Paradise. Portrait of the wrestler El Gallo wearing Mexican rings.

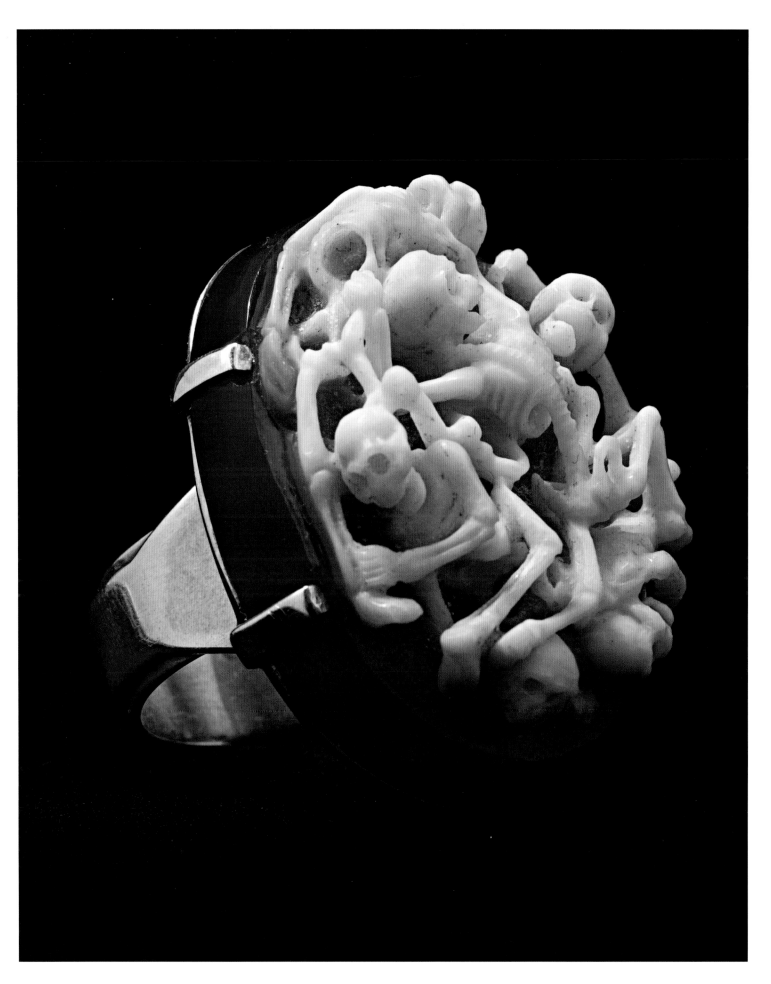

Left: Two skull rings with crossed pistols, Heart of Jesus, Crystal Evolution. **Right:** Masterpiece of fine sculpting, round funeral ring, cameo, yellow gold, one-of-a-kind, Marc Gassier, 2014.

Left: Vampire meeting. Vanitas skull rings in silver and metal. Upper left to right: graphic skull, metal; SS mask, skull inscribed into the iron cross. Bottom: Ernesto Che Guevara skulls (left) and Dracula (pointed canines and full eyebrows). **Right:** Chemical Attack. Vanitas skull rings. Top: skull ring, skull ring with facets, 1970s-1980s; Middle: helmeted skull, yellow gold, 1970s; Bottom: gas mask ring, Abraxas; vanitas skull in rhinestone and enamel. **Following double page spread:** Ring tray. Biker rings, silver-plated metal, United States, G&S. "An extremely high-quality sample from my collection, with exceptional and unique subjects in a Hells Angels style."

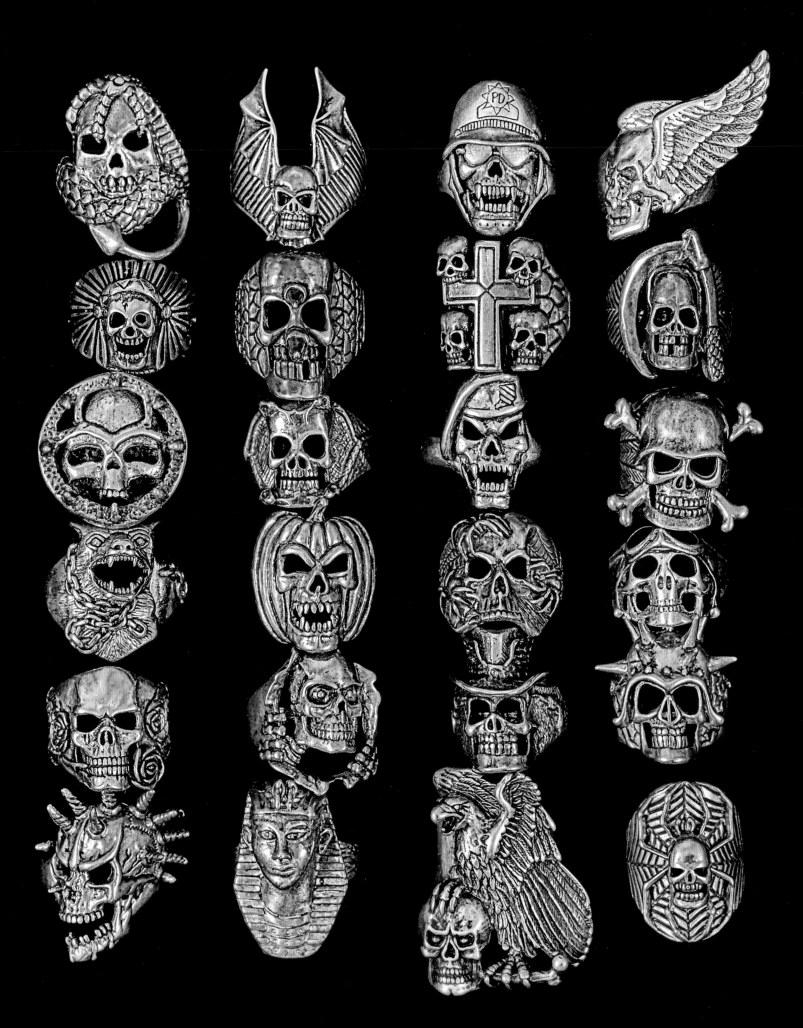

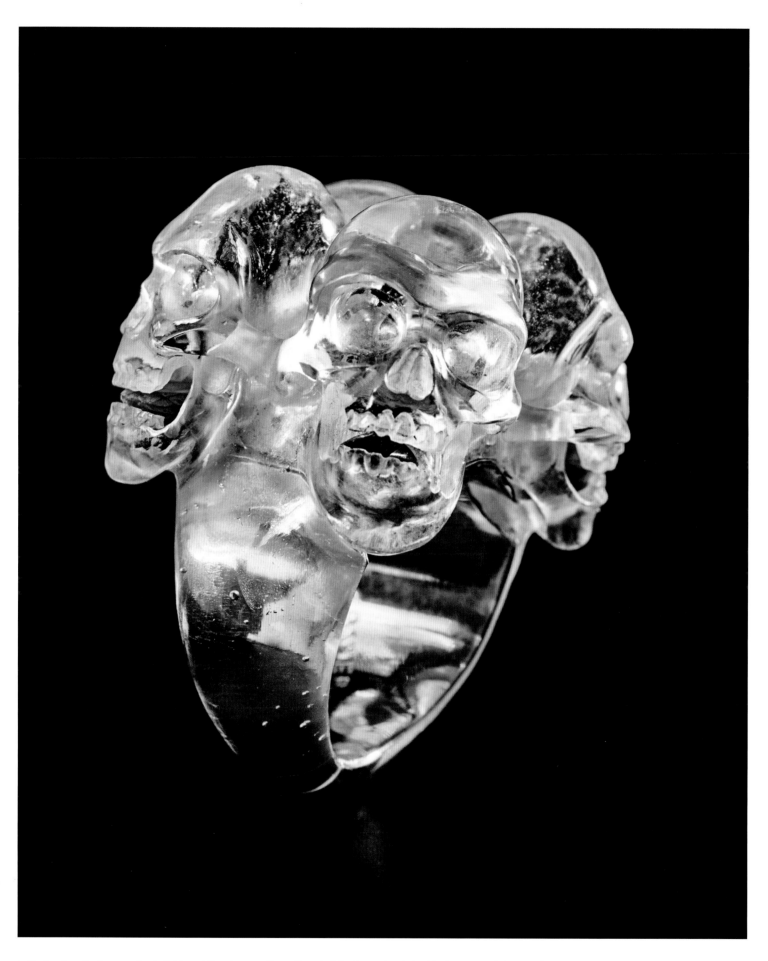

Left: Death with flowers, the knight and the dragon. "A vanitas skull in the style of the Mexican Day of the Dead with a joyful face!" Vanitas skull rings, circa 1980–1990. On the ring's shoulder, St. George slaying the dragon, hand embossed yellow gold, amethyst, Malta. **Right:** "A truly rare designer ring done in a 19th century style." Macabre carousel. Four vanitas skulls on the bezel, crystal, round brilliant cut semi-precious stones set into the jawbone, yellow gold setting, one-of-a-kind, Marc Gassier.

Left: Cemetery dance. Four vanitas skull rings, silver. Front left: blood vessels enameled in red on the forehead, eye sockets set with crystals. **Right:** Our Father. Clockwise: batwings holding a heart, black crystal, metal, Alchemy Gothic; skulls with spiders, United States; skull with Ottoman helmet, silver; pewter skull.

Left: "When I wear one of these rings, it takes me back to the flying saucer films of the 1970s." Hockey mask of Jason Voorhees, serial killer from the horror film *Friday the 13th*. Alien ring, silver and crystal, 2000s. **Right:** Traces. Rings, "Amu" (vanitas skull) and starry flag, Christ on the cross engraved on the shoulder, collage of onyx, pink quartz, and white quartz, M.A.R.S, Japan.

Left: Spider-vanitas skull with blindfold, weaving his web to capture his prey. Assortment of five silver vanitas skull rings, Abraxas. **Right:** A circle of death... assortment of silver vanitas skull rings, 1970s. Top left: skeleton ring and enamel flags, silver, Tobias Wistisen, L'Éclaireur. Center right: pirate flag, skull and crossbones.

Left: *Star Wars*, droid image. "Little skeletons dancing, but by wearing them and touching them they feel quite joyful." Embossed, yellow gold, amethyst, hematite, topaz, Marc Gassier, 2000. **Right:** Gospel. Collection of silver biker rings, 1970s: skulls with snakes; skeletons holding a candlestick; hippie vanitas skull with a marijuana leaf and a peace sign, sailor's skull eaten by a mermaid, skeleton with legs and arms spread. **Following double page spread:** Ring tray. Biker rings, silver-plated metal, United States, G&S.

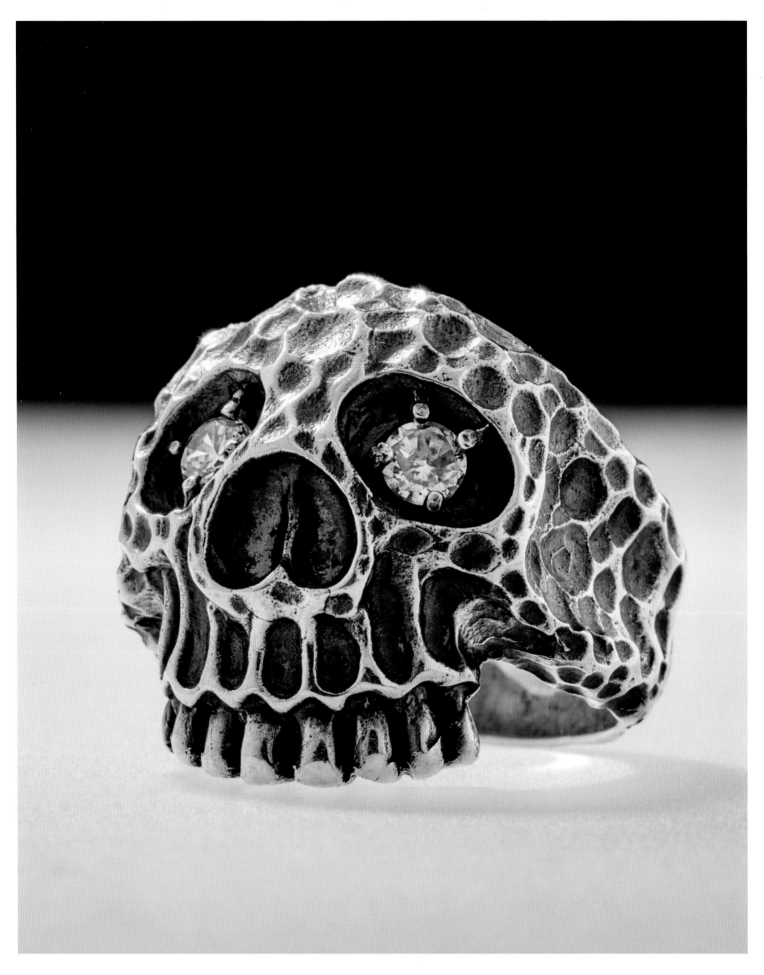

Left: Flamboyant vanitas skull, silver and rhinestone. **Right:** "Worthless but effective!" Vanitas skull rings in silver and metal. Diagonal to the right, top to bottom: aviator; monkey skull; circle of skulls holding a synthetic gemstone, Alchemy Gothic, 2004.

Left: Hells Angels rings, motorcycle skeleton, motor, biker, American biker ox skull, silver, G&S. **Right:** Maori warriors. Assortment of vanitas skulls, scarred and
tattooed skulls in flames, silver rings, 1980s.

Left: Metallic art. Vanitas skull ring, Bubonic plague, granulated silver, polished and rough, Alina Alamorean, 2011. **Right:** "Damien Hirst before his time", silver, diamond paving, blackened wood, Christian Breul Von Maria.

Left: Sparkling vanitas skull meditating on the cross. Rings, silver, crystal, Crystal Evolution. **Right:** Shrunken heads. Assortment of vanitas skulls. Clockwise: accumulation of skulls; smooth skull; fireball skull sticking its tongue out; vanitas skull with crown and bone collection on the shoulder, Abraxas; vanitas skull with the tibias crossed and a bowtie, red resin.

6

ETHNIC
& TRAVEL
SOUVENIRS

The rings of this category are an invitation to travel, a tour of the world in 90 objects, a dive into the heart of the cultures of all five continents. By following in the footsteps of the greatest explorers, silk road merchants, adventurers of the Citroen expeditions, and contemporary ethnologists, Gastou delivers a personal version of the world as he discovers it. His ethnic rings become archaeological objects, ritual paraphernalia, and commercial artifacts destined for tourism or the synthesis of a dialogue between populations.

The archeological exploration of Africa, colonialism and religious missions of the 19th and 20th centuries brought the art and crafts work of Africa to the world. Orientalist artists portrayed the populations they encountered. The Tuaregs, a nomadic people, inspired great curiosity and were painted by Etienne Dinet, Jean-Leon Gerome and Jacques Majorelle. They became known as "blue men" for the color of their cloaks, or "the Lords of the desert" for their art of war. Tuareg blacksmiths primarily craft in silver. They are known for their necklaces in the shape of an Agadez cross, of which there are more than 20 local varieties, and also engraved rings with abstract geometric patterns that include ebony insets and Goulimine glass beads (p. 228), a kind of token money made from colored glass.

South of the Sahara, the French lieutenant Louis Desplagnes was the first to study the Dogon people. His work was furthered by the ethnologist Marcel Griaule in the 1930s, promoting their cosmogony and sculpture throughout Europe. Masks and statues are found in Dogon jewelry. Characters, animals and symbolic elements are represented in bronze; warriors on horseback (p. 224) for the clan chief, a chameleon (p. 217) for the healer, and the mythical antelope and protector of the sun. These rings are indicators of social function, territories or a religion. The duck (p. 237), that perfect balance between water, air, and earth, presented majestically on a disk of water, is similar to the earrings worn by the Lord of Sipán discovered in Peru in 2015 and on the two rings which are displayed in the Louvre attributed to Ramses IV. Ancient Egypt was also a significant source for jewelry. The archaeological work undertaken in the 18th century brought this art forward from the past. The Egyptian revival style adorned both furniture and ceramics with new designs. The construction of the Suez Canal between 1859 and 1869 heightened interest for Egyptian-inspired art and historical-looking jewelry. The discovery of Tutankhamun's tombstone by Howard Carter in 1922 offered a lavish vision of the age of the pharaohs. Among the decorations found in the tombs, historians discovered thousands of objects in the shape of a scarab—sacred animal and a symbol of the sun's movement as well as a good luck charm. The scarab could be mounted on a ring with a rope décor (p. 205) which turned to reveal an inscription engraved on its stomach.

Throughout history, merchants have crossed great distances, spreading cultures far and wide as they traveled. The incense route between Egypt and India, the Silk Road between the Byzantine Empire, Central Asia, and China, and then the spice route over the oceans are examples of the constantly increasing exchanges between societies. Coins, art objects, and technologies all traveled. That exchange can be seen in this ring engraved with the words, *"Il-la-ah"* (For Allah) dated from the 9th century and exhumed in Sweden, a true connecting link between Sweden and the Islamic caliphates.

Toward the east, the lapis-lazuli cabochons of Afghanistan were combined with the intensity of "meenakari" enamel, produced in India under the Mughal Empire. These dynasties of enlightened rulers promoted the development of the arts—from architecture to stone and metal work—foreshadowing the jewelry of the maharajas. The aesthetic of these jewels inspired the European designers of the 20th century like the Cartier brothers and Jeanne Toussaint, to whom we owe Cartier's panther logo, as well as Van Cleef & Arpels, Mauboussin and Madame Boivin.

Hindu and Buddhist gods, like Ganesh (p. 214) and Buddha (p. 211) also appear on rings. These figures became popular during the hippie movement of the 1960s, especially in the United States. This pacifist counter-culture movement also celebrated Native American rings. The movement went from Indian lapis-lazuli to the most luminous turquoise blue. This precious stone, cherished by early Amerindian societies, was used by the Navajo Indians to satisfy a significant jewelry market demand in the 1970's, beautifying the faces of native American Chiefs and majestic eagles (p. 230-231). Today, jewelry designers work with the same stones and find inspiration in the same pantheon of sacred figures, like the Zuni Indians of New Mexico with their stunning minimalist rings (p. 212) or the sculpture rings featuring Quetzalcoatl and the jaguar warrior (p. 202) with his terrifying face mask. Like the sailors who returned home covered in tattoos, like writers Cendrars, Kessel and Lévi-Strauss who crafted their passionate travel narratives, like artists Matisse, Picasso, Breton and Frida Kahlo who were inspired by indigenous arts, and like fashion designers Paul Poiret, Elsa Schiaparelli, and Yves Saint Laurent who focused on traditional clothing, Yves Gastou looks for the beauty of the object in each country he has visited, to ensure that "statues die, too[1]" is something that never comes true.

Harold Mollet

1   Title of a documentary by Chris Marker, Alain Resnais, and Ghislain Cloquet, 1953.

Left: Aztecs. Top: ring featuring Quetzalcoatl, the feathered snake, founder of Mexico, silver, Mexico. Bottom: jaguar warrior ring, Aztec military elite, silver, Mexico. **Right:** Jewish wedding ring, silver, Germany or the Rhineland area, circa 1900. Building-shaped in the style of a synagogue or the Temple of Jerusalem. The ring has an opening mechanism on the engraved inscription: "Mazel Tov!", meant to give the newlyweds a favorable star alignment. This ring belongs to an Ashkenazy tradition dating from the Middle Ages. In the Sephardic culture the shape is different and looks more like a ring decorated with Byzantine jewels. The ring is only worn by the bride during the marriage ceremony; after the wedding it can be worn around the neck.

Left: Travel souvenir ring featuring Kâla, bronze, Indonesia, Java, early 20ᵗʰ century. Kâla is the god of death and destruction and is often found at the entry to Hindu temples. **Right:** Egyptomania. Scarab rings, Egyptian revival, gold, silver, metal and stone, early 19ᵗʰ century and 1920-1930s, became popular after the discovery of Tutankhamen's tomb by Howard Carter in 1922.

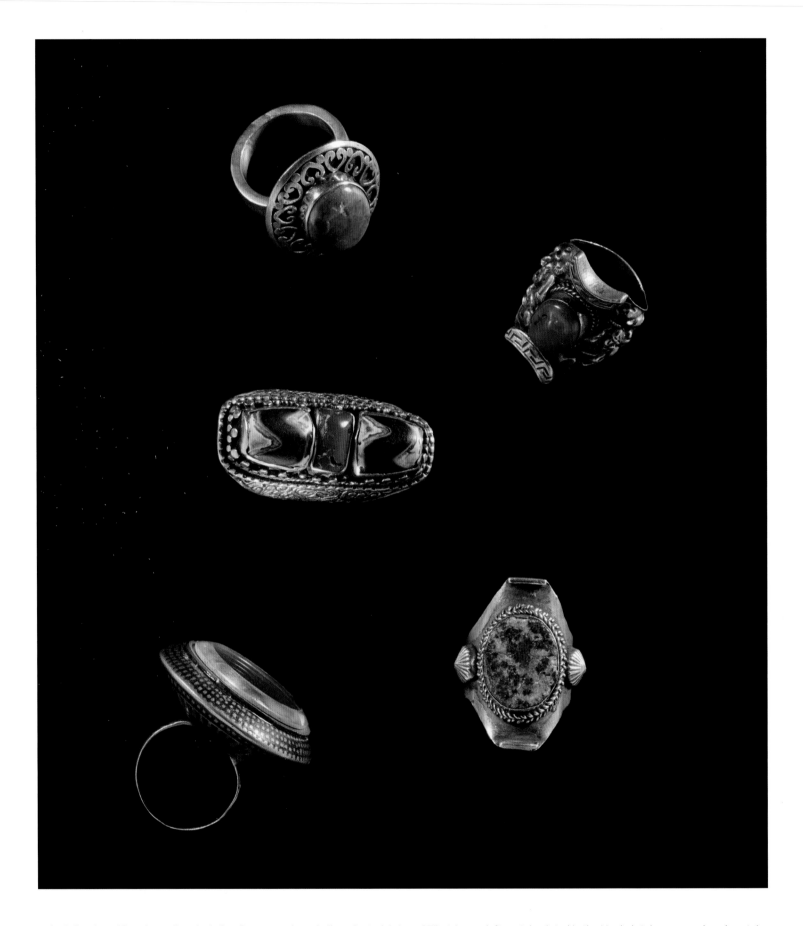

Left: Collection of five rings, silver, lapis-lazuli, agate, red coral, silver, Central Asia and Tibet. Lower left, metal painted in the Mughal style, concave bezel containing soil hidden by cut glass, Penjab, Pakistan. **Right:** "Around the world souvenirs." Clockwise: Ring, silver, verses from the Koran engraved on the bezel, Maghreb or Iran. Silver, mounted coin, Iran. Silver and vermeil, calligraphied and filigree Arabic writing, the Magreb or Iran. Engraved ring, oriental work. Souvenir ring from Egypt, silver, circa 1930. This image of Cleopatra wearing the double crown (Upper and Lower Egypt), holding the cross of life and facing Horus, the god with the falcon head, is a copy of the reliefs of the temple of Dendera. Ring, stylized mask, Mexico. Representative of "otherness", the ethnic ring is a symbol of the constant exchanges between people, but also of the crisscrossing of knowledge, languages and both religious and secular symbols. Arabs, Muslims, Persians, Jews, Berbers, Europeans, and the Chinese all created—through jewelry—commercial links and connections enriched by other relationships with the Mediterranean world: Ottoman Empire, Malta, France, Portugal, Italy, Spain.

Left: Tuareg and Bedouin rings, granulated silver, filigree, incised and embossed, hard stone, Morocco, Yemen, Mauritania, Mali. **Right:** "As someone who loves sculpture, I adore wearing these rings." Chief's ring, shield, bronze, Africa.

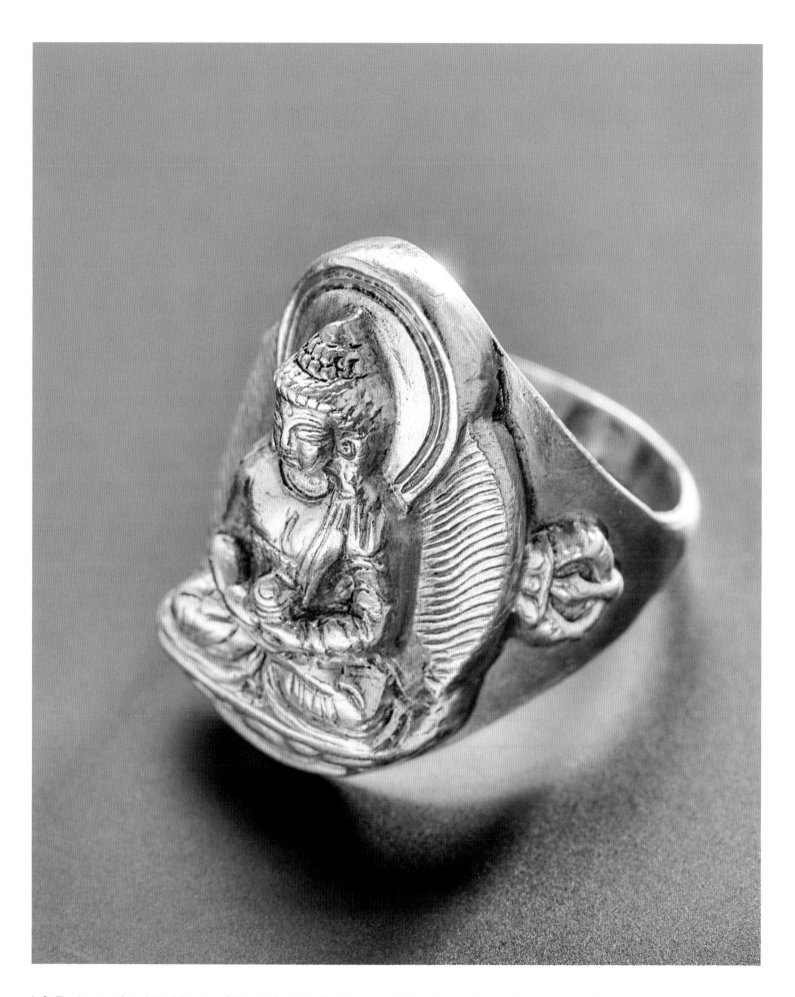

Left: The Japanese brand M.A.R.S is one of Gastou's favorites. They are now collector's items and impossible to find today. *Sixth* ring, silver, collage of amethyst and ivory, 2003, M.A.R.S. **Right:** "Souvenir from Kathmandu. All the beatniks brought back this kind of ring." Silver, meditating buddha, Asia, circa 1970.

Left: Rio Grande. Mosaic of turquoise, onyx, aventurine, agate, tiger's eye, alpaca, Zuni craftsmanship, New Mexico, Arizona, North Mexico, 1970s. **Right:** Celtic. Two rings, silver-plated and gold-plated metal, love arrow and moonstone, openwork foliate scroll pattern; Foreground, Art Nouveau revival ring, silver, hematite, La Mandragore.

Left: Ganesh, bronze, India, circa 1970. The elephant god, symbol of wisdom and intelligence, is one of the most popular of the Hindu pantheon. **Right:** "Even if these stones are only glass, the settings are done in a finely embossed silver. They are really Bollywood!" Silver and colored glass, except for the one on the upper left whose setting is composed of a block of malachite set with semi-precious stones (citrines and pink topaz), India, 1950–1960s.

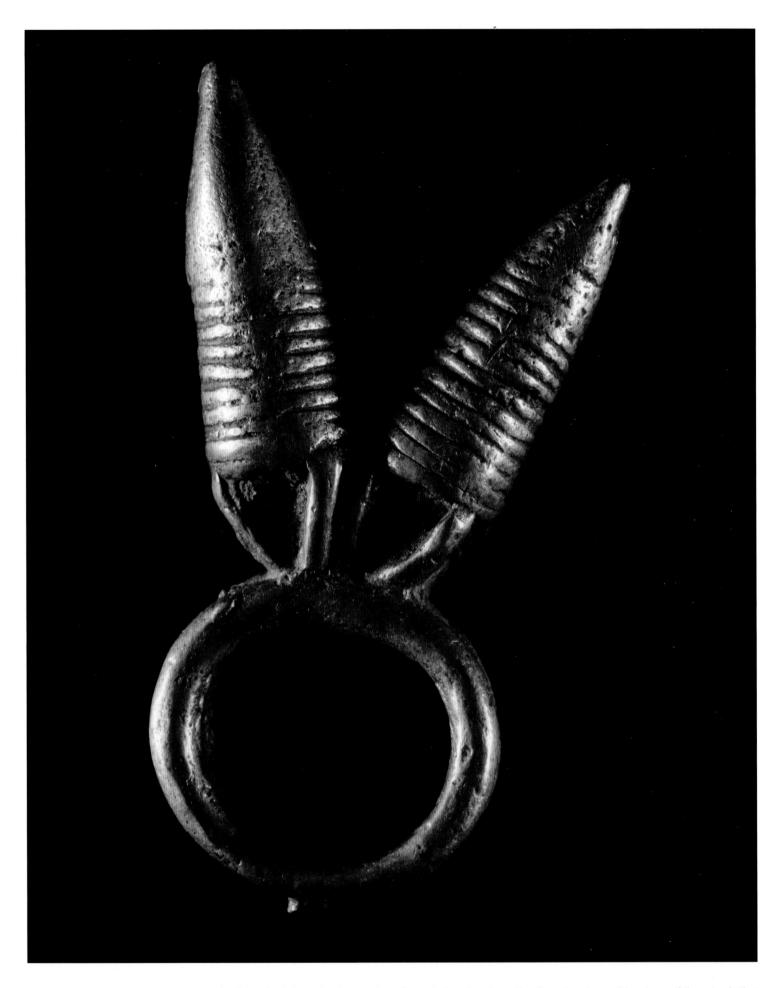

Left: Dogon double-cone ring, bronze, Mali. **Right:** Chameleon ring, bronze, Ivory Coast. In Senufo culture, the chameleon is considered one of the animals that
is an intermediary between the human and the spirit realm.

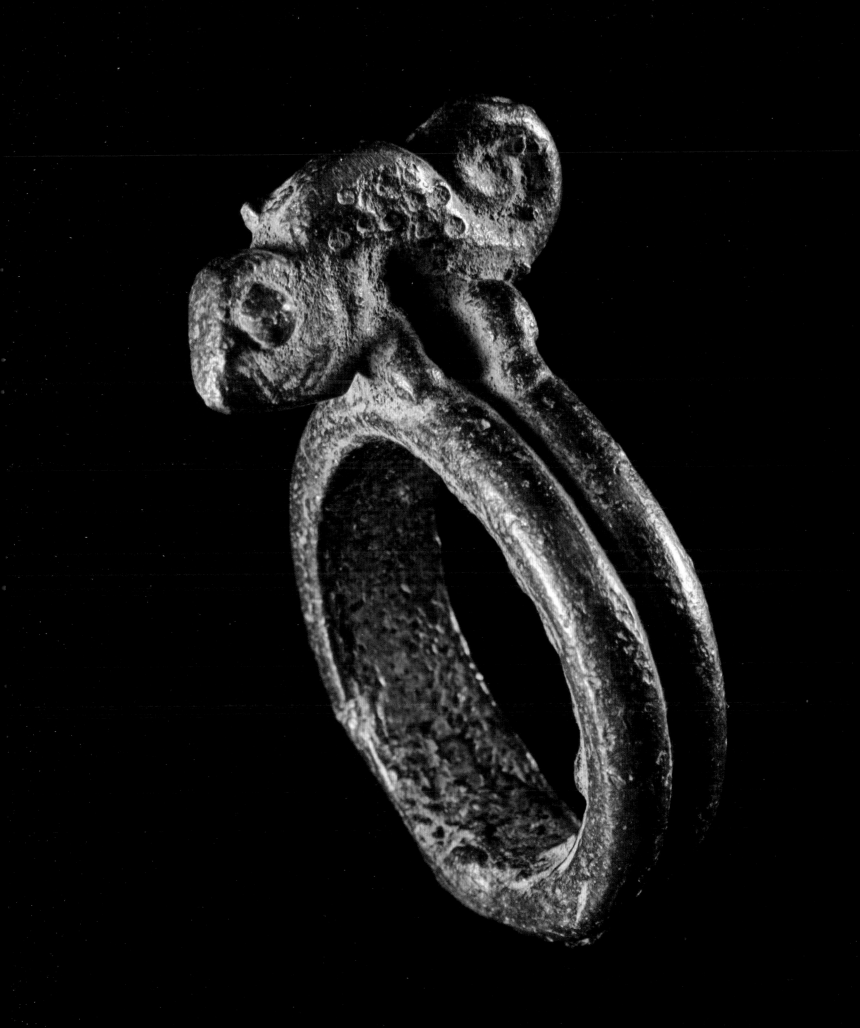

Left: Native. Native American rings, silver and turquoise *sleeping beauty* rings, United States, 1970. Upper left, mosaic of turquoises characteristic of the work of Navajo Indians, Arizona. Middle right and bottom, rings with a floral motif from the Pueblo region of Colorado. **Right:** Jaguar god. Navajo rings, turquoise and red coral, engraved and granulated silver, New Mexico, circa 1970. Mexican rings, Mayan character, horseshoe, food, alpaca and mosaics of opal and tiger's eye, circa 1970. Jaguar papercutting knife, gray gold paved with hematite and ruby, precious wood, Mellerio dits Meller, circa 1950.

Joey Starr wearing his rings.

Left: The secret of the mummy. Two rings, souvenirs from Egypt, carnelian, turquoise and silver, 1960s; tiger's head ring, silver, 1960-1970. **Right:** "It's Byzantine!" From left to right on the Elvis belt buckle: Neo-byzantine rings in granulated vermeil, cut amethysts, spiral filigree on the shoulder, Hilat; lower left, engineer's ring with owner's name (Herman Gren) and date (May 20, 1959) engraved on the ring; center, signet ring, blood jasper, yellow gold, custom ordered one-of-a-kind, Cartier, 1968; right, Neo-byzantine ring, cabochons of garnet, amethyst, tourmaline and fine pearls in a rose pattern, guilloché and granulated gold, 1900.

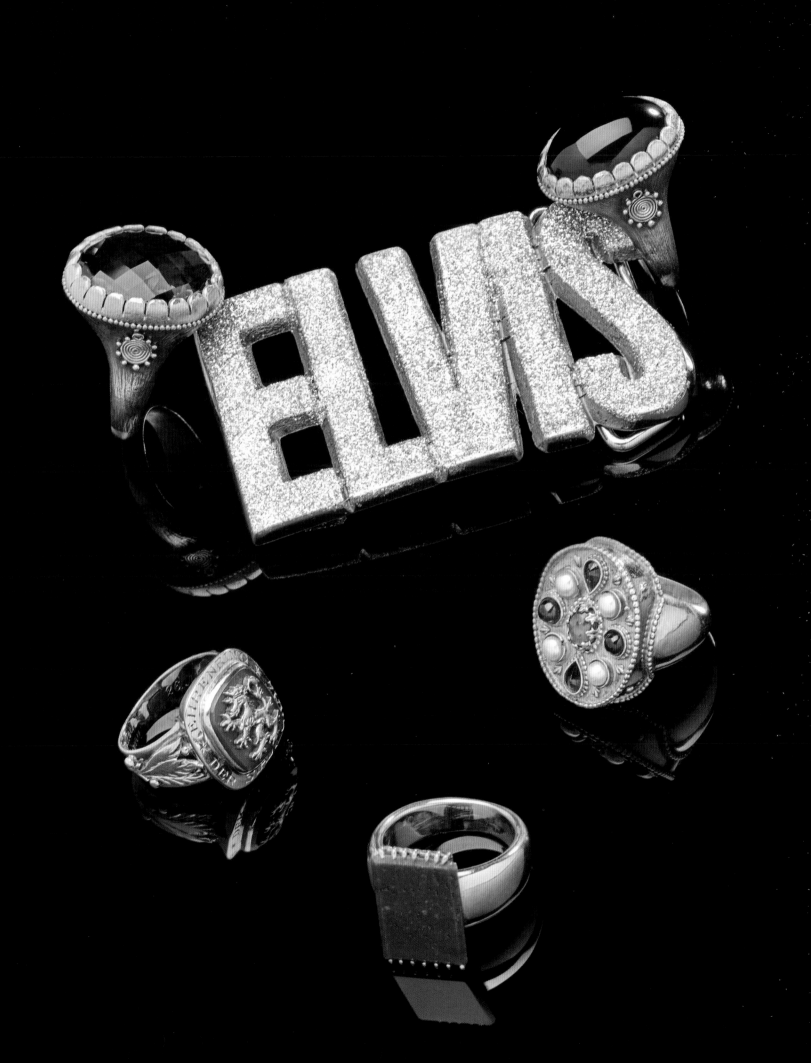

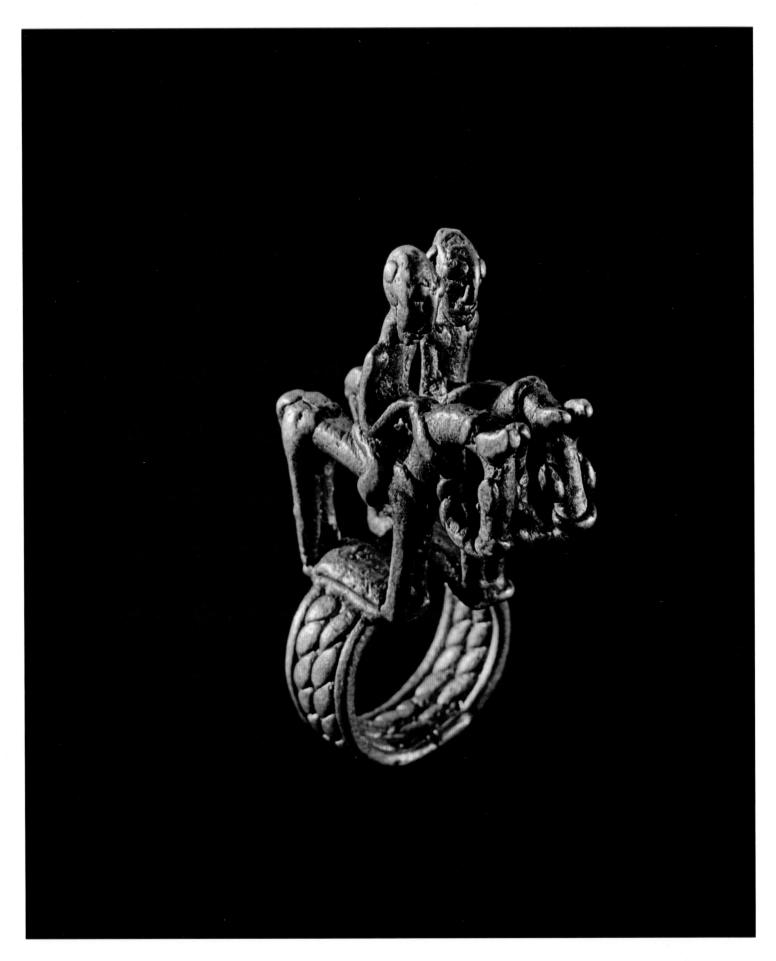

Left: Dogon horsemen rings, bronze, Mali. This prestigious ring was worn by the Hogon, the religious chief, the blacksmith or other nobility. **Right:** Top: Berber ring, granulated silver and glass; Tibetan coin from the 12ᵗʰ century set in yellow gold. Middle right: vermeil and agate cabochon, image of *makara* on the shoulder. The makara is a creature associated with fertility in the Hindu bestiary. Middle left: silver and gold ring, carnelian intaglio. Bottom: seal ring, granulated and filigree silver, Iran.

Left: Rings from archeological digs like those found within the Châlus treasure. Pinky rings, bronze, Roman and Gallo-roman. Their shapes are evocative of the Byzantine prototypes from the heights of the Middle Ages which were commonly found from the Balkans to England and also some Venetian rings of the 14th and 15th centuries. **Right:** Eye-catching. "It's such a shame that the tradition of belonging to a university or a club doesn't exist in France. Men would have been able to wear more rings." University and military rings, polished silver and vermeil, glass and enamel, United States, circa 1960-1970.

Left: "Tuareg jewelry is extremely beautiful and worn so well by their men with their incredible style, wrapped in their turbans and long cloths. Sober and powerful, these rings represent their essence perfectly." Assortment of Tuareg rings from the Sahara region, silver engraved with stylized motifs, ebony, Goulimine bead, 1950s and 1960s. Upper left: Goulimine bead set in the center of the oblong bezel, Mauritania. Goulimine bead looks like an eye and so is associated with medicinal qualities. **Right:** "There is no clash of civilizations, but a meeting of civilizations." Abderrahmane Sissako, author and director of the film *Timbuktu*, 2014. On the stone: ring in yellow gold and aventurine, Turkey, 1950s; silver ring, openwork floral motif on the shoulder, tiger's eye, Southeast Asia, circa 1930. Around the stone from left to right: silver ring, antique piece with a verse from the Koran on a starry background, re-mounted in the 1930s probably by a European; Tuareg ring with a lovely, nearly futuristic setting which would not be out of place in a science fiction film; Chinese coin mounted in the 1930s in silver, most definitely a travel souvenir. **Following double page spread:** Born in the USA. Ring tray. American rings, silver-plated metal, enamel, encrusted with turquoise in the style of a Hopi mosaic, G&S.

Left: Chief's ring, onyx, bronze, Africa. **Right:** Mask ring, bronze, Africa.

Left: Central Asia, silk route journey and crossroads of the civilizations. Three seal rings from Central Asia, turquoise (Turkmenistan or Uzbekistan) and carnelian intaglio featuring a horse (Afghanistan). Two hippie rings, European craftsmanship from Buddhist inspiration. **Right:** Super Bowl. American football championship ring, 2001, New England Patriots. The ring offered to the winner is made up of 42 diamonds to symbolize the 42-year history of the team; the two baguette cut diamonds symbolize the shape of the Super Bowl trophy, and the navette cut for the football; the enameled section (red and blue) is for the Patriot's helmet; the date and the year of the trophy are on the shoulder in numbers and in relief, United States.

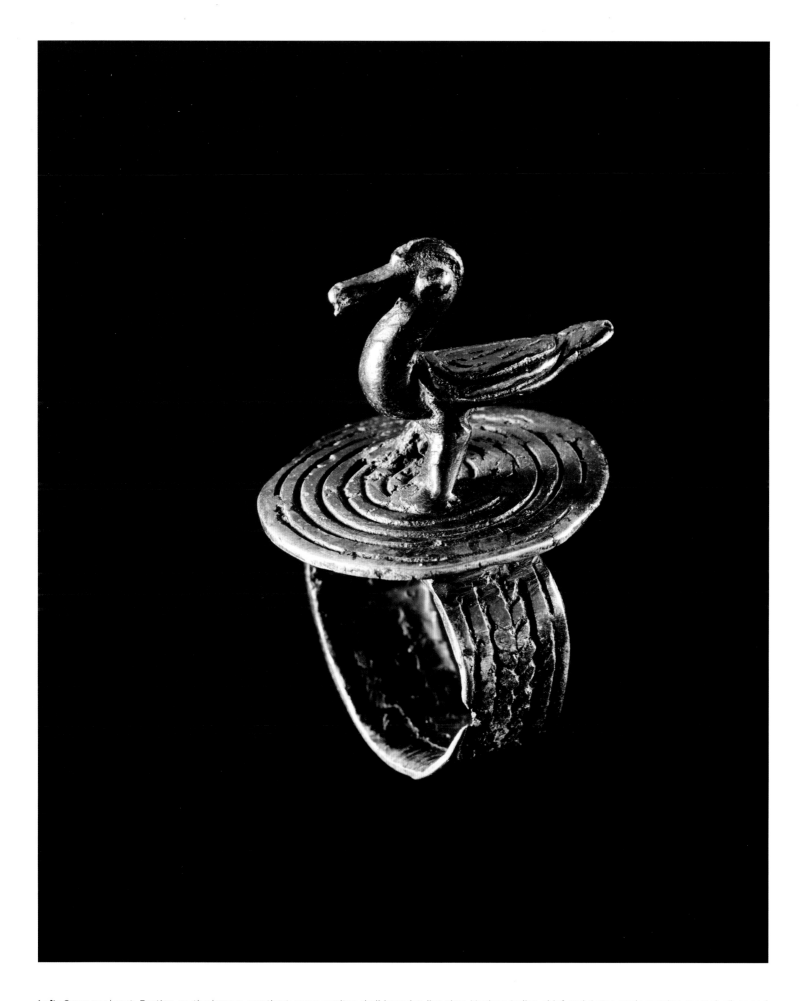

Left: Cross my heart. Resting on the bronze amethyst cross: vanitas skull bracelet, lion ring, Mexican Indian chief and Aztec eagle warrior, enamel, silver and turquoise and coral mosaic. **Right:** Bird ring, bronze, Ivory Coast. The sacred symbolism of the Senufo associates the bird with heavenly and agricultural powers.

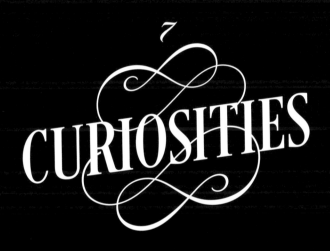

7

CURIOSITIES

A collection is a cabinet of curiosities, where codes are broken and preciousness rubs shoulders with simplicity, where refinement and kitsch remain side by side. The gray area between costume jewelry and masterpiece of goldsmithing is where Gastou's vision of beauty resides. The profound social transformations of the beginning of the 20th century and the constantly increasing improvement in the means of production induced a paradigm shift in the jewelry arts. Alongside fine jewelry appeared a new kind of jewelry—where the ring becomes an original sculpture or an object of consumption.

Starting in 1890, Art Nouveau moved away from historical traditions and upended the art of the jewel. Artisans became artists, much like René Lalique. They took their inspiration from nature and created a new formal language and a freedom from ornamentation. They used stones, pearls, and glass to highlight the metal bed, itself skillfully worked. This first break with classical rules only developed further with the dynamism of the avant-garde. From surrealism to new realism, from pop art to narrative figuration as well as minimalist art, all of the great names of the 20ths century got interested in jewelry, creating a miniature version of their artistic world and their palette. With its sensual element, jewelry is often meant for a particular individual: Man Ray for Catherine Deneuve, Calder for Peggy Guggenheim. "There is no art form more intimate, it can be worn and touched," says Diana Küppers. Rings, broaches, earrings are all unique creations, like certain pieces by Lucia Fontana, or produced in a small series, like the pins designed by Roy Lichtenstein. Artists joined up with jewelers and goldsmiths like François Hugo did with Pablo Picasso. The Italian publisher GEM, founded by GianCarlo Montebello in 1967, created jewels for about 50 major artists, including Ettore Sottsass, César and Pol Bury. Alongside these highly limited productions, the major brands also contributed to the spread of artist jewelry, from the mythic *Trinity* ring created by Cocteau for Cartier in 1924, to Robert Indiana's *LOVE* ring for Ultima II cosmetics in the 1970s and the B.ZERO.1 collection by Anish Kapoor for Bulgari in the 2010s.

In their never-ending quest to beautify the body and their sentimental relationship with objects, artists "certainly enrich what could be called a sensitivity to the material, the introduction of contact with surfaces, knowledge gained through touch," (Emmanuel Guigon). Yves Gastou has something of this philosophy as a dealer of fine antiques, but also in his exploration of the sculpture ring, from raw crystals (p. 272) to the pure refinement of Henri Gargat and his *Tourbillon* ring (p. 272).

Baudelaire talked about the eroticism of the jewel in *The Flowers of Evil*: "Ce monde rayonnant de métal et de pierre / Me ravit en extase, et j'aime à la fureur /

Les choses où le son se mêle à la lumière." (This radiant world of metal and of gems / Transports me with delight; I passionately love / All things in which sound is mingled with light[1]) and this reached its apogee during the sexual revolution of the 1960–1970s. Gastou's ring featuring a naked woman with her wrists tied behind her back (p. 299) is reminiscent of Allen Jones's provocative furniture, while the engraving of a Plexiglas ring (p. 153) hints at Gotlib's comic drawings and prefigures the X-Ray series from the early 2000s by Wim Delvoye.

While remaining as personal as the others, Gastou's fantasy rings are derived from a broader image base and reference both cultures and popular icons. Fantasy creatures decorate his rings, a menagerie escaped from a Füssli painting, Grimm's fairy tales, the playful films of Hayao Miyazaki as well as slave and Chinese mythologies. The collection includes gargoyles and gothic bats, Asian dragons, Nordic wolves and wild boar, reptiles, animal skulls and American eagles, hunting trophies, hybrid creatures, and monsters and amulets. The images are both realistic and abstract, like the elk ring by designer Thomas V (p. 249).

In our image-based society, adornments also become an evocative product: an object symbolizing a fictional character; Ridley Scott's *Alien* on a ring featuring a decomposing body (p. 294). Sometimes only one element is enough to identify the reference—Goldorak's helmet (p. 246), Predator (p. 271), Spiderman's mask, or even just Mickey Mouse ears. Walt Disney Studios created the character in 1928 and became the first derivative product with Mickey Mouse watches in 1932. An American star, his silhouette has been appropriated by artists like Warhol and André Saraiva with his *Mickey Viagra*, by designers like Pierre Colleu with his Mickey and Minnie dressers, and by the world of fashion in Adidas sneakers and Marc Jacob's t-shirts. His evil twin was used in street art (p. 289) and also appeared in a short film in 1995 called *Runaway Brain*.

With this part of the collection, Yves Gastou delivers a complete vision of the world of masculine jewelry, something between the quest for a one-of-a-kind piece and passion project in which every design deserves attention and finds a place on his hands. Just as Oscar Wilde once said: "One should either be a work of art, or wear a work of art."

Harold Mollet

1   Translation by William Aggeler, *The Flowers of Evil* (Fresno, CA: Academy Library Guild, 1954).

Left: "As a child I loved climbing bell towers. I can finally wear a gargoyle." Legendary creature ring, silver and crystal, Crystal Evolution, 2010–2015. **Right:** "The Jesus heart, the heart of love and also, yes, the flame because of our dreams." Jesus heart ring, Crystal Evolution.

Left: Between the claws of an imaginary creature... Silver rings, 1980-1990, Abraxas, ibid, p. 58. **Right:** "A worrying bat, a vampire..." silver ring, La Mandragore.

Left: Superheroes. Goldo Fuck Finger Ring, re-appropriation of the famous manga Goldorak, by the street artist Pimax, silver, Abraxas edition. **Right:** Thracian gold. "One of the gems of my collection. Large ring done in the style of the jewelry worn by the Thracians, an ancient people from the Balkans. They were well-known for the richness and finesse of their goldwork. Engraved stone in a setting of two deer with their antlers crossed, granulated and filigree gold, 19th century.

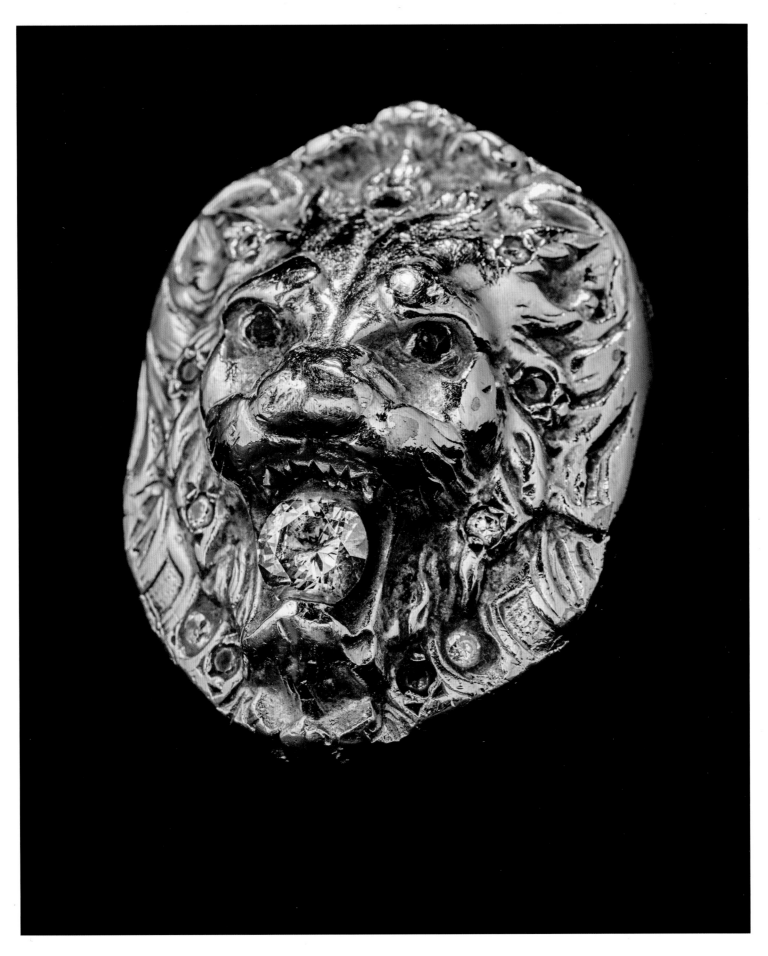

Left: The king of Gypsy jazz. Lionhead ring that once belonged to Django Reinhardt, bronze, synthetic gemstones, circa 1945–1950. The guitarist himself offered the ring to the antique dealer, Michel Vogelhut, after a concert at the mythic jazz café on the rue des Rosiers near the Saint-Ouen flea market, a symbol of friendship and the passion for jazz that both men shared. **Right:** Serial killer deer. Sculpture of the Prince of the Forest by Mellerio dits Meller; on the left antler, deer ring and sado-masochistic Mickey, Thomas V. blackened surgical streel; on the right antler, hip-hop monkey skull with headphones.

Left: St. George and the dragon. Mascaron and winged dragon ring, silver, circa 1960. **Right:** Theory of Evolution. Falcon vs eagle. Left: Rebel and heart ring featuring a falcon, silver, zirconium oxide, onyx, Thomas Sabo, 2015. Right: biker ring: *Wild Eagle SOA Motorcycle*, metal, G&S, United States.

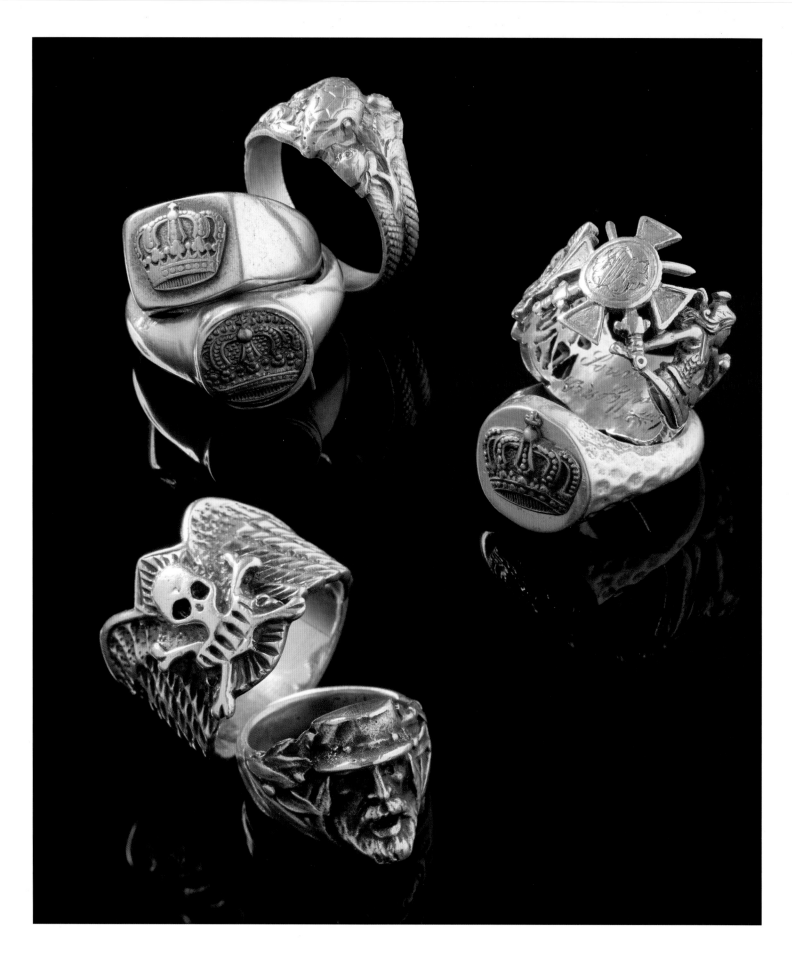

Left: Men in the trenches. Collection of French soldier-made rings, created using the aluminum of French and German bomb casings, 1914–1918. The rings featuring the crown of the German Empire were the work of German soldiers. Other symbols are otherwise typically French: a soldier's head set between palm fronds, Marianne with cuirass and wearing a Phrygian hat, dedication in French engraved inside the ring, snake and Lorraine thistle symbolizing the lost country to take back from the enemy. The skull and crossbones is a universal symbol, evoking death and the long shadow it casts. **Right:** Born of tears and blood. On a silvered bronze relief featuring a suffering Christ, bat (Alchemy Gothic), dragon, bird skull (Marc Gassier), gorilla, wolf, and scorpion rings.

Left: "Opera rings, to wear when listening to beautiful music." Lower right: vanitas skull ring, silver and bronze. Middle: fragment of a meteorite set into a ring, silver, Côté Mecs (left); ring decorated with the crown of the sultan of Oman (Qabus) on the shoulder and the bezel, silver and glass, Sultanate of Oman (right). Back: theatre ring, pompon, mother-of-pearl, setting with flowers and fleur-de-lis, circa 1900; ibid. p. 264–265. **Right:** Strange bestiary. On the helmeted judas shield, webbed foot rings, snakes, crowned frog, bat, pitbull.

Left: Evolution spin. Neanderthal meets Homo sapiens. Ring of partially reconstructed hominid on the skull, silver, 1970–1980s; truncated pyramid ring, silver with black enamel, M.A.R.S., Japan; blackened silver ring, circular band in black crystal, Swarovski. **Right:** From bottom to top: armory ring in platinum and diamonds; ball ring, silver, cap encrusted with onyx, Alan Crocetti, 2015. From left to right: vanitas skull rings, Crystal Evolution, G&S. **Following double page spread:** Wild. Ring tray. Wild animals and popular alternative figures (Indian chiefs, shamans, pharaoh, Samurai), silver-plated metal, G&S.

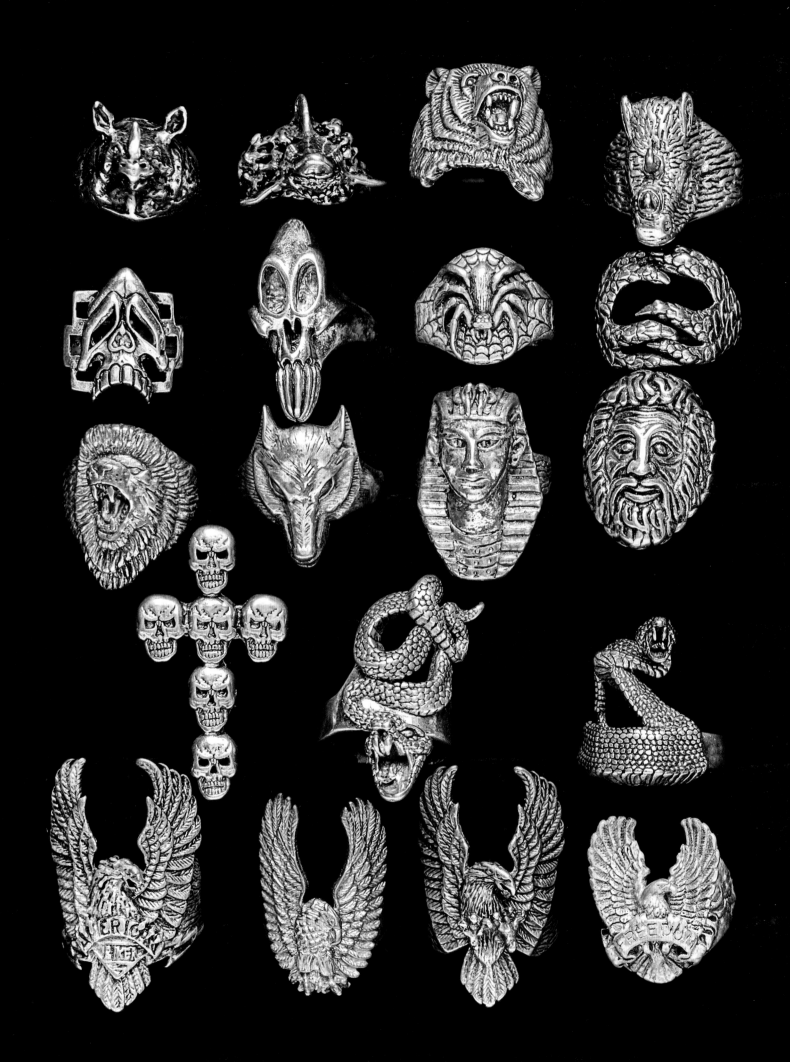

260   **Left:** Crazy horse. Horse skull head, gaping jaw, silver, Marc Gassier, 2011. **Right:** Luxury viper. Two rings, snakes, silver, 1980–1990s.

Left: "Haunted house: my dream! And the enchanted cemetery: my childhood walks." *Vision II* rings, engraved silver, Théo Mercier, produced by Le Buisson. 2013.

Right: Celestial. Engraved vanitas skull ring; ring, black onyx with white quartz star inlay, crucifixion on the shoulder, silver, M.A.R.S., Japan.

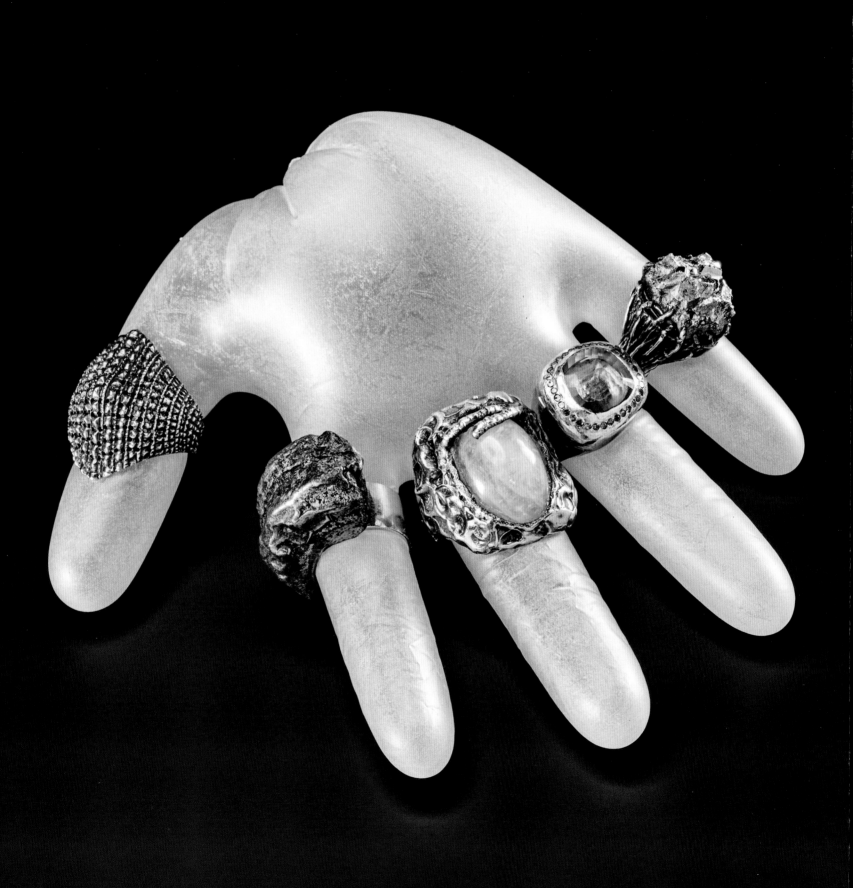

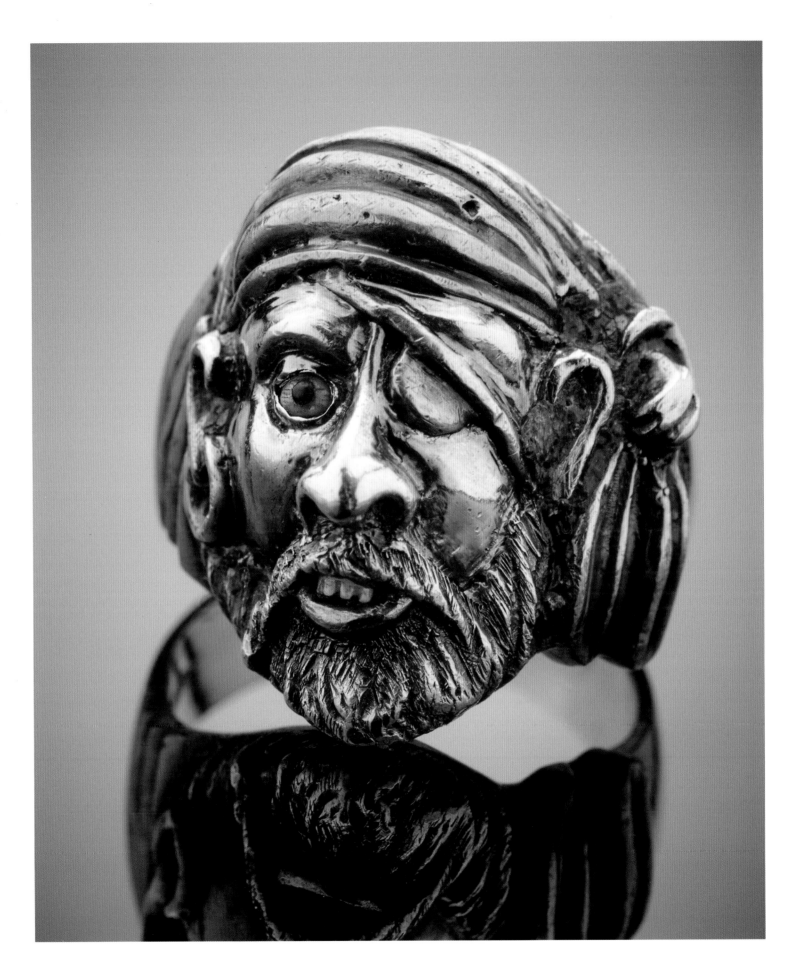

Left: Spectral Dandy. Thumb: granulated silver ring set with gemstones, Ugo Cacciatori, L'Éclaireur. Ring finger: polished silver ring, stones, Rosa Maria, L'Éclaireur. Index: ring, piece of the robe of an antique bronze statue set into a silver band, Luigi Scialanga, circa 2000. Middle finger and ring finger: silver cast, pink agate and pyrite (ibid. p. 254), circa 1970. Typical of the hippie chic movement, these rings illustrate the era's renewed use of raw stones. **Right:** Red-beard. Pirate ring, sulfur eye, ivory teeth, silver (swan stamp, foreign origin), yellow and pink gold (scallop seal), custom ordered one-of-a-kind, first half of the 19th century.

Timour, sousaphone player. The amazing ring he wears was designed by one of his friends during a trip to Burkina Faso and made because of the Ouagadougou smelters competition that made it using pewter from old sinks. The ring is also a mini flask for hard liquor to drink during concerts...

Left: Werewolf ring, silver, 2000–2010s. Beyond its beautiful depiction of the theme, this ring is distinguished by its astonishingly delicate embossing for such a contemporary ring, Abraxas. **Right:** Animal skull ring, miniature goat skull, one-of-a-kind, numbered 1/1, custom ordered by Yves Gastou from the artist Marc Gassier, 2010.

Left: "Put them on your finger, you'll never take them off!" Departure for the world of science fiction. Space man meetings: Spiderman ring, silver and mother-of-pearl, 2010. **Right:** Ring inspired by the film *Predator*, silver.

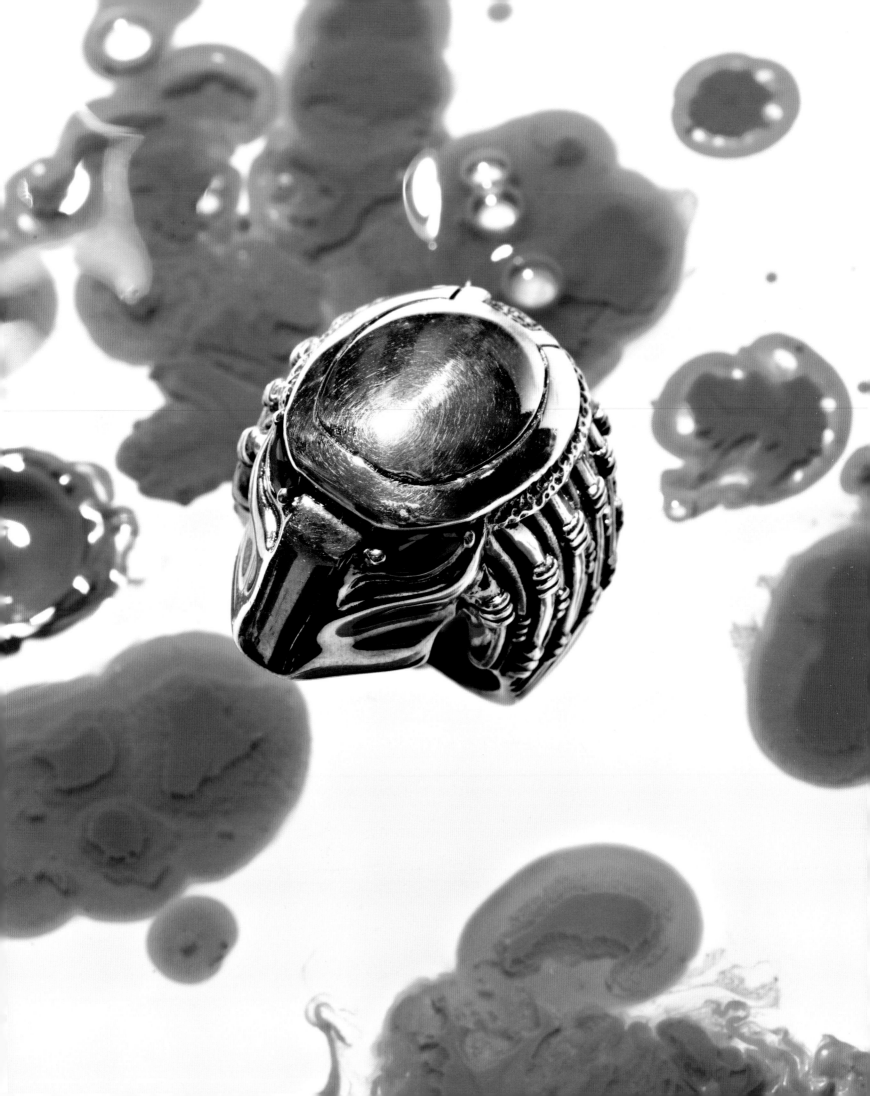

Left: "Really futuristic ring from the 1970s, combined with real technical prowess." Kinetic ring: *Tourbillon*, mobile puck on an axis, steel, Henry Gargat, 1972. **Right:** The temptation of hell. "Confrontation of two designer rings, one from the 1950s and the other contemporary." Two-finger ring, image of a geode, surgical steel, Thomas V, 2013. Centaur ring in ronde-basse, silver, Peter Vacori, 1950s.

Left: Clockwise: Prometheus ring, silver, Italian craftsmanship; ring of snake entwined on a finger, Romantic era; scarab ring, vermeil, semi-precious stone, 1900–1914; Art Nouveau ring in the shape of hand-crafted volutes, designer jewel, one-of-a-kind, circa 1900. **Right:** Divining arts. Dragon and bat rings, metal, circa 1970.

Left: *Sex in progress & rake's progress*. Perseus and Andromeda. Ring of a monster piercing a woman (Andromeda), solid silver, 1960–1970s. Winged dog ring (Perseus), flying to save her, silver, 1960–1970s. **Right:** "Another masterpiece of style." Machine skull, silver, one-of-a-kind, André Lassen, 2008.

Left: Comedia dell'arte. Two grotesque rings, bronze, circa 1900. **Right:** "Costume jewelry to awaken the dreams of future jewel lovers or collectors." Rings, vanitas skulls, dice, English flag, heart, Indian chief and cartoon characters, gold-plated and silver-plated metal with enamel.

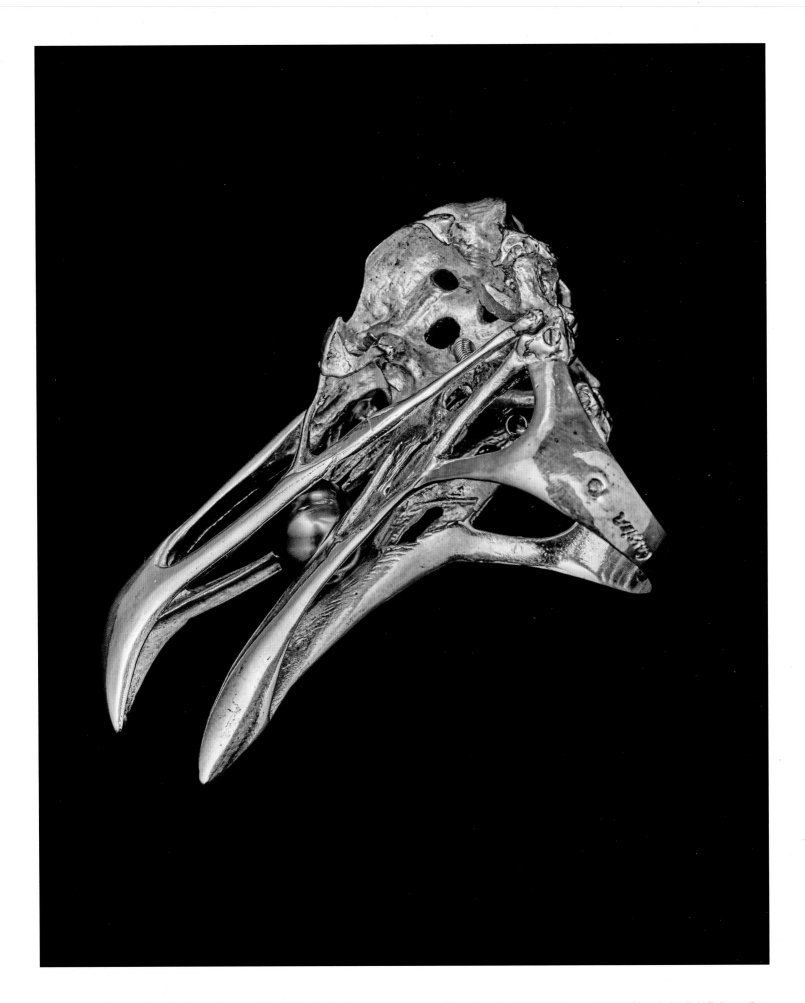

Left: Seagull. Seagull skull, black pearl from Tahiti set into the bird's open mouth, silver, Marc Gassier, 2012. **Right:** Fontaine's Fables. Animal skull rings, silver, yellow gold, cultured pearl, Marc Gassier, 2011. Bottom, left to right: bat and cat; center: seagull; top, left to right: horse and dog.

Left: "I once asked a sculptor to make me a ring. I was surprised sometime later when he brought me this unwearable insanity." Sculpture ring, steel, Guy Lartique, circa 1980. **Right:** Coils, entanglements, interlacings. Symbols of the ring: eternity, the immutability essence of things. From top to bottom: cross ring, silver, José Esteves, contemporary design; movable wedding rings, turning on an axis, silver and vermeil, Claire Wolfstirn, 2010; interlacing rings, ring with gourmette chain links, creeping vine ring, silver, striped band, partially blackened silver, Côté Mecs.

Nilko, graffiti artist (Loveletters, Bagarre), in his Oldsmobile, 1958. His graffiti ring, representing his NILKO tag and his Loveletters logo, was created by Anjuna, a
French jewelry designer, pioneer of hip-hop jewelry in Europe.

Left: What to do after God? Know how to bounce back. Top, sundial ring. Left, masonic ring, square and joined compass, symbols of the principles extolled by the Loges: "set their actions inside the framework of virtue." Right, fake clock ring in the shape of a decorated heart, 1970s. **Right:** Hosts of the city. Foreground: bee ring, silver; background: cat ring, silver enamel, Marc Deloche; spider ring, Alchemy Gothic; snake ring, silver, Abraxas. On the ramparts: lizard ring, silver, 1970s; inset spider ring, colored glass, Alchemy Gothic; octopus and elk rings, 1970s–1980s.

CARCASSONNE

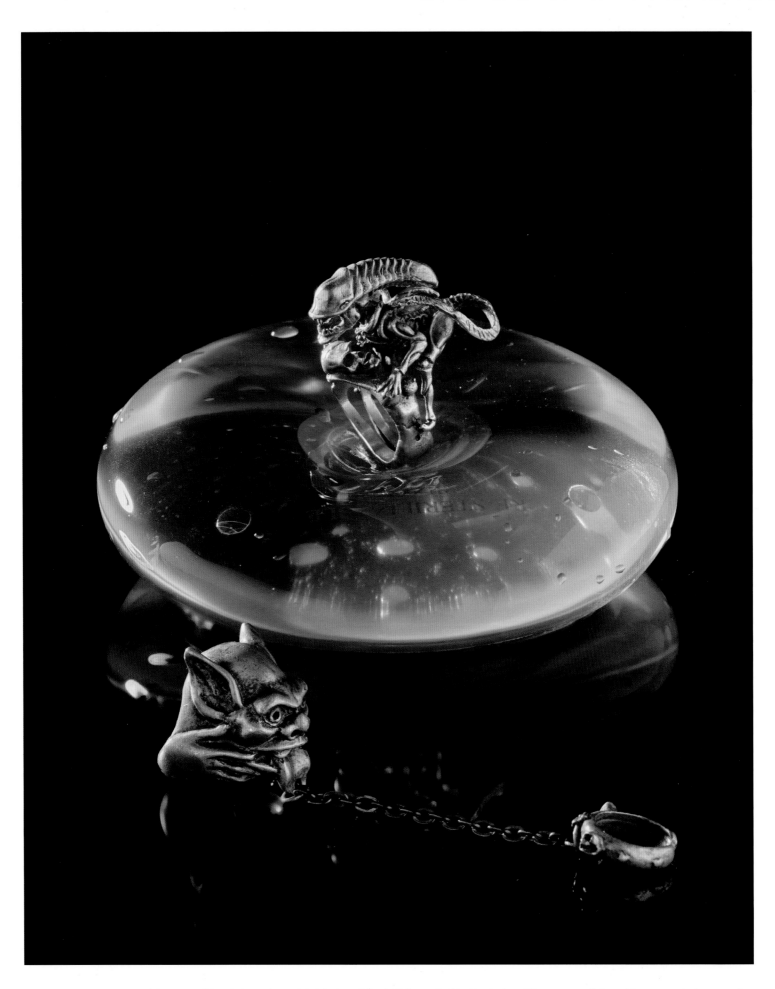

Left: Rape enticement. Double ring, troll head chained to a ring, blackened steel, Alchemy Gothic. Erotic ring, Alien monster flying with a woman's decomposing body, circa 1970. **Right:** Ferocious Mickey ring, silver, Abraxas, 1970–1980s.

288

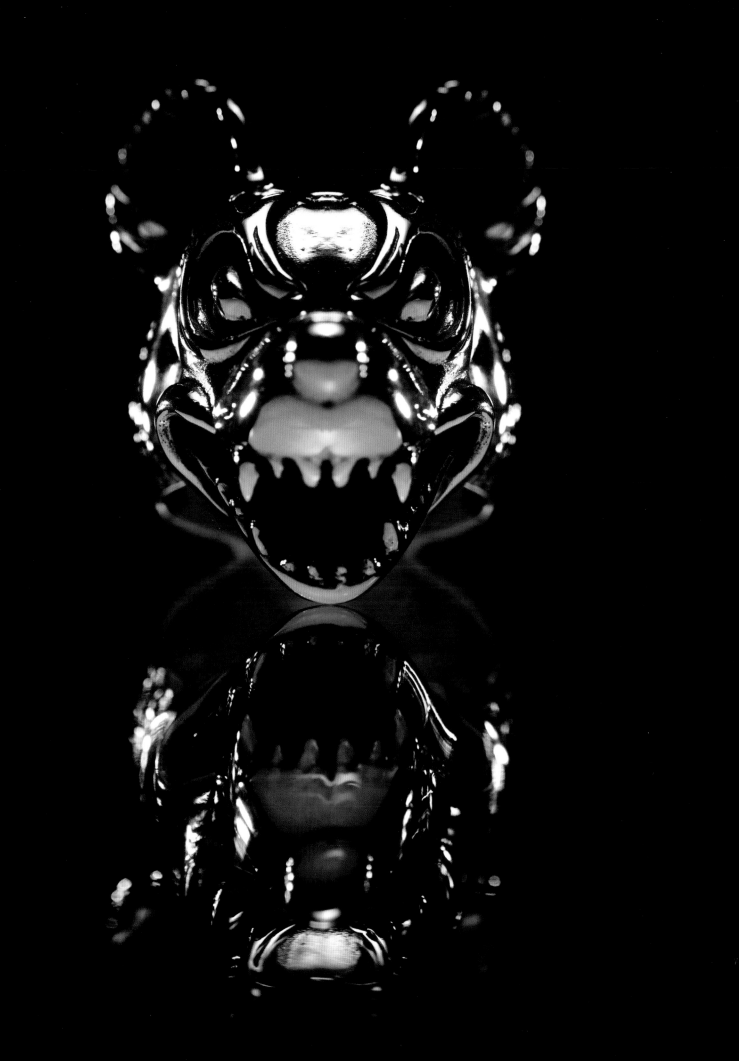

Left: Ideograms. *Old school* style rings, silver and enamel, star engraved on the shoulder, by the artist Wildcat for Abraxas. **Right:** Prickly. Clockwise: graphic skull ring, rhinestone, Mexico; ram ring, steel; gothic cross ring, vanitas skull ring, silver, Mexico, 1970-1980s.

Left: Dominant males. Bulls, rhinoceroses, crocodile and shark, circa 1970. **Right:** Biodiversity. Clockwise: scorpion, wolf, machine skull, ox skull, owl, silver, circa 1970s.

Left: Turning the tables. Civilization taken over by monsters. Romantic angel sculpture in bronze from about 1850 versus alien rings. **Right:** *Aliens—the return.* Monster ring in the style of the film, silver, 1980s.

Left: Secrets of the Louis XI torture chambers. Hanging in the chain links of the "Net": skull necklace, silver and stone, M.A.R.S, Japan. Ready to devour the cadaver of the torture victim: eel ring, silver, Laurent Esquerré, 2005. **Right:** Dance floor. Lion rings and scarred skulls, metal, contemporary designs.

Left: Eroticism and fetishism, from Jack the Ripper to Allen Jones. Clockwise: razor ring, England; corset ring, England; penis ring, silver, number 1/8, Bernard de Laméris, 2013. **Right:** "Between the objectified woman of the 1970s and the disturbed robot of the de-eroticized society of today, I choose the first because it reminds me of my own discoveries of the magazines *Lui*, with Aslan's drawings, and of *Playboy*, which I read under the covers as a teenager." Objectified woman ring, silver, England , 1970s; robot ring, silver and stones, Mia Fonssagrives-Solow, 2010.

BIBLIOGRAPHY

Antoine, Delphine. *Yves Gastou, antiquaire du future*. Paris: éditions Norma, 2011.

Barraud, M. l'abbé. *Des bagues à toutes les époques et en particulier de l'anneau des évêques et des abbés*. Paris: Derache, 1864.

Bizot, Chantal, Emmanuel Guigon, and Laurent Devèze. *Bijoux d'artistes.* Exhibition catalogue, musée du Temps. Paris: Hazan, 2009.

Bulletin de l'ANORAA, Association nationale des officiers de réserve de l'Armée de l'air, No. 63, 15 July 2016.

Cabanne, Pierre. *Les Grands Collectionneurs*. Paris: éditions L'Amateur, 2003-2004.

Deloche, M. "Le port des anneaux dans l'Antiquité romaine et dans les premiers siècles du Moyen Âge." *Mémoires de l'Institut national de France* 35, 2nd half, 1896.

de Sardes, Guillaume and Silvia Benedetti. "Codognato, orfèvre et collectionneur." *Prussian Blue*, March 2015. http://prussianblue.fr/codognato-orfevre-et-collectionneur/.

Didron, Adolphe-Napoléon. *Annales archéologiques*. Paris: librairie archéologique de Victor Didron, 1844.

Dulaney, William L. "A Brief History of "Outlaw" Motorcycle Clubs." *International Journal of Motorcycle Studies*, 1. No. 3. November 2005.

Freeway Mag, No. 177.

Gautier, Théophile. *A History of Romanticism*. Translated by F.C. Sumichrast. New York: George D. Sproul, 1908.

Heuzé-Joanno, Michèle. *Henri Gargat, l'empreinte*. Exhibition catalogue, Espace Solidor. Cagnes-sur-Mer: 2011.

Koudounaris, Paul. *Heavenly Bodies, Cult Treasures and Spectacular Saints from the Catacombs*. London: Thames & Hudson, 2013.

L'hospitalité. *Études*. Tome 408, 120 pages. Paris: S.E.R. éditions, 2008.

Lion, Antoine. "Art sacré et modernité en France: le rôle du P. Marie-Alain Couturier." *L'histoire des religions*, 1, Paris, 2010.

Matzneff, Gabriel. "Ma bague de Codognato." *Prussian Blue*, March 2015. http://prussianblue.fr/ma-bague-de-codognato/.

Pierrat, Emmanuel. *La Collectionnite*. Paris: éditions Le Passage, 2011.

Puissance du Gothique. *Sociétés & Représentations*. No. 20, 292 pages. Paris: Publication de la Sorbonne, 2005.

Quin, Elizabeth. *Le livre des vanités*. Paris: éditions du Regard, 2010.

Rheims, Maurice. *Haute Curiosité*. Paris: éditions Robert Laffont, 1976.

Rheims, Maurice. *La Vie étrange des objets*. Paris: éditions 10/18, 1963.

Rheims, Maurice. *Les Collectionneurs*. Paris: éditions Ramsay, 1981.

Venet, Diane, ed. *From Picasso to Koons: The Artist as Jeweler*. Milan: Skira, 2011.

Vever, Henri. *French Jewelry of the Nineteenth Century*. Translated by Katherine Purcell. London: Thames & Hudson, 2001.

BIOGRAPHIES

Benjamin Chelly has worked in Paris since 2001. He began his career working with silver print and was trained in Paris photo studios. His portraits were noticed by Paris's Festival d'Automne, which then hired him. He began collaborating with numerous newspapers, magazines, and institutions (*Le Monde*, *Les Échos*, *Transfuge*, *Danser*, *Vogue* and also *L'Odéon*). He then became interested in architecture and construction sites, as well as the workers at those sites. He also does advertising photography for art, tourism, and fine cuisine. The photography of objects, design, and jewelry completes his field of expertise and corresponds to his taste for technical precision and working with light.

Delphine Antoine is an art historian specializing in Art Nouveau and decorative arts. She is the author of numerous catalogs and several art books: *La Nudité dans l'École de Nancy* (Gérard Klopp, 2009) and *Yves Gastou, antiquaire du futur* (Norma, 2011).

Harold Mollet is a specialist in 20th century decorative arts and design and has developed an interdisciplinary approach toward history and art nurtured by his passion for film, theatre, and literature.

ACKNOWLEDGEMENTS

With warm thanks to: Delphine Antoine; Harold Mollet; Nicolas Bos; Benjamin Chelly; Marie Vallanet-Delhom; Anne Desnos-Bré; Pierre Léonforte; Victor and Mathilde Gastou, my children; Charles Jaigu; Anne Dressen and Olivia Gaultier for the exhibition *Medusa* at the Musée d'Art moderne; Olivier Lorquin for the exhibition *Les vanités, c'est la vie* at the Musée Maillol; Guy Boyer; Élisabeth Védrenne; Frédéric Gilbert-Zinck and the entire team at L'ÉCOLE, School of Jewelry Arts; Dominique Forest of the Musée des arts décoratifs; Éric Jansen, Valérie Duponchelle; Agnès Renoult.

Thank you also to: Aden (Gavilane); Michel Aliaga at Cartier; Xavier X; Pia de Brantes; Bernard Français; Armand Hadida; Francis and David Holder; Peter Marino; The Museum of Jewelry in Pforzheim, Germany; Nilko; Joey Starr; Franck Terem and the wrestler El Gallo; Jean-Michel Signoles and Laurence Grima; Sophie and Fred at the Gallery Acanthe, Jean-Louis Tapiau, Karine Berrebi, Lapo Elkann, José and Jackie Zago, Patrice and Odile Corbin, Didier Chabut and Valérie Lhomme.

Finally, I am very grateful to L'ÉCOLE, School of Jewelry Arts for the support they have given me.

Yves Gastou

Gingko Press Inc.
1321 Fifth Street
Berkeley, CA 94710 / USA
books@gingkopress.com
www.gingkopress.com

Gingko Press Verlags GmbH
Schulterblatt 58
D-20357 Hamburg / Germany
gingkopress@t-online.de
www.gingkopress.com

ISBN 978-3-943330-18-2

English Edition published under license from Albin Michel.
French original Edition © 2018 Albin Michel

Éditions Albin Michel
22 rue Huyghens
75014 Paris / France
nicolas.decointet@albin-michel.fr
www.albin-michel.fr

For the French Edition:
Editorial director: Nicolas de Cointet
Editorial assistant: Mihaela Cojocariu
Art director: Peruk
Design & Layout: Caroline Dauvois
Production: Alix Willaert

For the English Edition:
Translation from the French: Michelle Bailat-Jones
Proofreading: Christl Hansman
Design & Typesetting: Benjamin Wolbergs
Project Coordination: Anika Heusermann

Printed in China by Toppan Leefung